The Drug Scene

INQUIRY INTO CRUCIAL AMERICAN PROBLEMS

Series Editor · JACK R. FRAENKEL

The Drug Scene:

Help or Hang-up?

WALTER L. WAY, M.D.

University of California
at San Francisco

PRENTICE-HALL, INC.   ENGLEWOOD CLIFFS, N.J.

Titles in this series:

CRIME AND CRIMINALS: What Should We Do About Them?
Jack R. Fraenkel

PREJUDICE AND DISCRIMINATION: Can We Eliminate Them?
Fred R. Holmes

THE DRUG SCENE: Help or Hang-up?
Walter L. Way

POVERTY IN AN AFFLUENT SOCIETY: Personal Problem or National Disgrace?
David A. Durfee

COUNTRY, CONSCIENCE, AND CONSCRIPTION: Can They Be Reconciled?
Leo A. Bressler and Marion A. Bressler

VOICES OF DISSENT: Positive Good or Disruptive Evil?
Frank Kane

CITIES IN CRISIS: Decay or Renewal?
Rudie W. Tretten

TEEN-AGERS AND SEX: Revolution or Reaction?
Jack L. Nelson

PROPAGANDA, POLLS, AND PUBLIC OPINION: Are the People Manipulated?
Malcolm G. Mitchell

ALIENATION: Individual or Social Problem?
Ronald V. Urick

EDUCATION AND OPPORTUNITY: For What and For Whom?
Gordon M. Seely

FOREIGN POLICY: Intervention, Involvement, or Isolation?
Alvin Wolf

THE ENVIRONMENTAL CRISIS: Will We Survive?
Charles B. Myers

POPULATION AND SURVIVAL: Can We Win the Race?
Jack L. Nelson

VIOLENCE IN AMERICA: What Is the Alternative?
Jack Zevin

AMERICAN WOMAN TODAY: Free or Frustrated?
Elsie M. Gould

Prentice-Hall International, Inc.
London
Prentice-Hall of Australia, Pty. Ltd.,
Sydney
Prentice-Hall of Canada, Ltd.,
Toronto
Prentice-Hall of India Private Ltd.,
New Delhi
Prentice-Hall of Japan, Inc.,
Tokyo

13-220814-8 paper
13-220842-2 cloth

PREFACE

The series *INQUIRY INTO CRUCIAL AMERICAN PROB-LEMS* focuses upon a number of important contemporary social and political issues. Each book presents an in-depth study of a particular problem, selected because of its pressing intrusion into the minds and consciences of most Americans today. A major concern has been the desire to make the materials relevant to students. Every title in the series, therefore, has been selected because, in one way or another, it suggests a problem of concern to students today.

A number of divergent viewpoints, from a wide variety of different *kinds* of sources, encourage discussion and reflection and illustrate that the same problem may be viewed from many different vantage points. Of concern throughout is a desire to help students realize that honest men may legitimately differ in their views.

After a short chapter introducing the questions with which the book will deal, Chapter 2 presents a brief historical and contemporary background so that students will have more than just a superficial understanding of the problem under study. In the readings that follow, a conscientious effort has been made to avoid endorsing any one viewpoint as the "right" viewpoint, or to evaluate the arguments of particular individuals. No conclusions are drawn. Instead, a number of questions for discussion and reflection are posed at the end of each reading so that students can come to their own conclusions.

Great care has been taken to insure that the readings included in each book are just that—readable! We have searched particularly for articles that are of high interest, yet from which differing viewpoints may be legitimately inferred. Whenever possible, dialogues involving or descriptions showing actual people responding and reacting to problematic situations are presented. In sum, each book

- presents divergent, conflicting views on the problem under consideration;

- gives as many perspectives and dimensions on the problem as space permits;

- presents articles on a variety of reading levels, in order to appeal to students of many different ability levels;

- presents analytical as well as descriptive statements;

- deals with real people involved in situations of concern to them;

- includes questions which encourage discussion and thought of the various viewpoints expressed;

- includes activities to involve students to consider further the issues embedded in the problem.

CONTENTS

5   Opinions About Drug Usage   72

6   What Should Be Done?   86

Introduction

Speed kills
It really does
Amphetamine,
Methedrine, etc.
Can and will, rot your
teeth, freeze your mind
and kill your body. The
life expectancy of the average
speed freak, from the first shot
to the morgue, is less than five years.
What a drag.

This is one view of what is often referred to these days as the "drug problem." Here are some other ideas: From two college students:

Drugs . . . are only a means of feeling love (in the general, perhaps Christian sense) in this debacle of self-destruction . . . it is a return to Eden . . .

I have stopped taking drugs. . . . It became all too easy to "groove" on something . . . without ever coming to terms with real problems, without ever really thinking. The border of illusion and reality becomes hazy.

From poet Allen Ginsberg: "Marihuana is a charmingly harmless herb."

From a message written on a mailbox in the Haight-Ashbury District of San Francisco, California: "Speed kills, but lack of speed produces lethargy."

Confusing, contradictory statements? They certainly are. Nevertheless, there is little denying that the use of such compounds is increasing, particularly in that segment of the population between 15 and 25 years of age.

A report from the Yale University Student Health Center reveals that one in five students has used "hallucinogenic" drugs [1] at least once.

A California high school survey of 19,000 students shows that one-third have used marihuana, LSD, or an amphetamine on at least one occasion.

A Haight-Ashbury drug dealer estimates that at least a ton of "grass" (marihuana, or marijuana) is consumed per week in San Francisco.

Such statistics certainly attest that drugs are being used. But they do not tell us why or by whom. The whole drug problem has burst upon the American scene with an impact that few would have predicted. Some feel that the use of drugs is detrimental, while others argue just the opposite.

A schoolteacher advocate says the following:

Marihuana is not harmful, to my knowledge, because I have been using it since 1949, almost daily with only beneficial results.

It has a relaxing effect when tension is present, my depth perception has been increased. . . . I do not consider marihuana an habit-forming drug but to me narcotics are. I have been smoking one or two marihuana cigarettes every evening, sometimes more if school is not in session when I stay up late at night.[2]

A former Harvard Professor, Timothy Leary, fiercely defends the place of psychedelic drugs in our society:

Three years ago on a sunny afternoon in the garden of a Cuernavaca villa, I ate seven of the so-called "sacred mushrooms" which had been given to me by a scientist from the University of Mexico. During the next five hours I was whirled through an experience which could be described in many extravagant metaphors but which was above all and without question the deepest religious experience of my life.[3]

On the other hand, authorities have issued grave warnings on the dangers of marihuana. The following is from a police department pamphlet:

Prolonged use of marihuana frequently develops a delirious rage, which sometimes leads to serious crimes. . . . Habitual use

---

[1] Drugs capable of causing a variety of psychic and perceptual changes including hallucinations, visual illusions, decreased concentration, change in mood, and anxiety.
[2] Marin County (California) *Independent Journal,* October 7, 1967.
[3] Timothy Leary, *The Psychedelic Reader,* G. M. Weil, Ed., New Hyde Park, N. Y.: University Books, 1965.

of this narcotic poison . . . causes a very marked mental deterioration and sometimes insanity. While the marihuana habit leads to physical wreckage and mental decay, its effects upon character and morality are even more devastating. . . . Moreover, even small quantities can destroy the will power and the ability to connect and control thoughts and actions thus releasing ALL inhibitions viciously.

A professor of the State University of New York, Dr. M. Cohen, states that LSD [4] may not only produce detrimental psychologic effects (the so-called "bad trip"), but that it also may cause chromosomal damage in the offspring of the mother who used the drug during pregnancy. Says Dr. Cohen:

> The consequences of the chromosomal imbalance may not appear for several generations. The total damage caused by LSD to the human population, both genetically and psychologically, therefore, may not be assessable for some time to come.[5]

Newspapers on many college campuses attempt to explain the advantages in using such drugs and to negate opposition. Here is a quote from one West Coast college edition:

> A few scientific lies about LSD and marihuana need to be discussed to prevent further cultural panics—like the one set off last year by a scientific "report" on chromosome damage by LSD—and to point out the gullibility gap between the ears of the public. . . .
> Lies spread fear, fear spreads the already deep misunderstanding people have of drugs. Drugs can be just as good or as bad as the way they are used. We should not be afraid of drugs but instead understand them because they can be helpful if used when necessary.[6]

And yet many people have never used drugs. Why not? The world of drugs is for many a remote area, best left alone. A number of doctors, professors, and social workers agree that the medical and legal consequences seem too severe to risk using drugs. Others, however, insist that there is something to be said for drug usage. One thing is certain: there are many questions that just cannot be put aside. For the nonuser: Should I give drugs a try? Am I denying myself a realm of experience by being closed-minded about drug use? What might happen to my health? How right would anyone be who tried to punish me for using drugs?

---

[4] Lysergic acid diethylamide. An extremely active hallucinogenic drug.
[5] M. M. Cohen, *et. al.,* "In Vivo and In Vitro Chromosomal Damage Induced by LSD-25," *New England Journal of Medicine,* 277:1043, 1967.
[6] Excerpted from Paul Kangas, *Open Process* (San Francisco State College Newspaper), February 20, 1968.

For the user: What exactly have drugs given me? Can I do the same things that I could do before using drugs? Can I do them as well? Might not this drug thing get out of hand? Is the use of drugs innocuous or not?

Many drugs are known to have powerful and far-reaching effects on those who take them. What kinds of drugs are used? What are their effects? How significant are these effects? Is the concern about drugs exaggerated and way out of proportion to the actual incidence of drugs? What is the significance of a California high school survey which showed that over one-third of the high school students in the county had used marihuana, LSD, or the amphetamines?

This book is designed to help you consider questions like the above. In particular, we will explore the following:

1. What are drugs?
2. What is the nature of the drug scene?
3. What causes the drug scene?
4. What is the extent of drug usage in this country?
5. How do various people feel about drugs and their use?
6. What effects have drugs had upon individuals and upon our society as a whole?
7. What might be done about drug usage?

In the chapters that follow, you will be presented with a variety of facts and opinions on drugs that should help you to form some conclusions of your own as to the nature and extent of the drug problem in American society today. A glossary is provided on page 111 to help you with any unfamiliar words or expressions, both technical and slang.

How Long
Have
Drugs Been Used?

How extensive has the use of drugs been in the past? Where have they been used? By whom? It is often implied that the use of drugs is a new phenomenon, peculiar to contemporary society. But there can be little doubt that the use of drugs has been going on for a long time. Let us very briefly consider the history of some of the better known drugs today—in particular, some narcotics (opium and cocaine); some amphetamines (Methedrine and Dexedrine); and some hallucinogens (marihuana and LSD).

OPIUM

The Sumerians cultivated the opium poppy plant five thousand years before the birth of Christ in order to extract its juice. The juice coagulated and was scraped from scars made the preceding night in the poppy heads. The Babylonians not only inherited Sumerian civilization, but also spread knowledge of the poppy's medicinal properties eastward to Persia. Knowledge was also spread westward to Egypt where this "poppy juice" (opium) was used to treat human ailments as early as 1550 B.C.

The opium poppy has been used for hundreds of years in many parts of the world. Archaeological evidence shows Assyrian physicians using it as early as 700 B.C., and the early Greeks used opium during the third century B.C. The Greeks associated the effects produced by opium with a sort of religious experience, as the writings of Homer illustrate:

> Chained with that virtuous draft, the exalted mind
> All sense of whoe delivers to the wind
> Though on the blazing pile his parent lay,
> Or a loved brother groan'd his life away,
> Or darling son, oppress'd by ruffian forces

5

Fell breathless at his feet, a mangled corse;
From morn to eve, impassive and serene,
The man entranced would view the dreadful scene.

In the *Iliad,* Homer wrote that the poppy had the power of "inducing forgetfulness of pain and the sense of evil." Virgil, the Roman poet, referred to the poppy in the *Aeneid,* and poppy seed sprinkled with honey over food was a Roman favorite.

It seems likely that the Greeks passed on their learning about opium to Arabian physicians, who helped the drug to become well known throughout the Middle East. Arabian traders introduced the drug to the Orient during the Tenth Century, where it was originally employed in the treatment of dysentery. Both Moslem and Christian Arabic doctors used it freely in their cures, and large numbers of individuals died of overdosage. It should be noted that until 1100, the drug was mainly used for medicinal purposes.

Opium also found its way to India where Barbosa, who travelled with Magellan, wrote in 1511 of the "opium which most of the Moors and Indians eat." The Chinese sailed to India to obtain opium, and thus began the opium "traffic" which we refer to today.

Opium was by no means unknown to Western Europe, however. In the 1500's, many physicians claimed that the drug would aid resistance to deafness, asthma, coughing, colic, jaundice, fever, leprosy, female troubles, melancholy, and the effects of poison. In 1803, Frederick Sërturner, a German, discovered morphine—an alkaloid of opium—and in 1898, heroin was developed from morphine.

The psychological effects of opium were noted in most of the aforementioned places but it wasn't until the 1700's that the use of the drug became prevalent entirely for its effects on the mind. The traffic in opium increased five-fold between 1729 and 1769, and the practice of opium smoking quickly became popular and profitable, as shown in this excerpt describing the practice of smoking opium in the Orient:

The great extent to which this destructive vice is carried on . . . together with the almost utter impossibility of relinquishing the dreadful habit, when once acquired, opens an immense source of revenue to the East India Company, who monopolize the sale of all quantities of opium. . . . The annual average revenue of this monopoly, . . . for ten years past, has amounted to 4822 £. [pounds] sterling [$11,572.80]. But the quantity of opium smuggled is immense and incalculable. . . .

It is well known now, that in several of the southern provinces of China opium is cultivated to a great extent, without any check from the local authorities. . . . The propensity to opium-smoking is becoming so universal and so irresistible in China, that no sumptuary laws, however sanguinary, will be able to stem the torrent. In Penang excessive duties have only increased the thirst for opium; and what is worse, they have quadrupled the number of murders and other crimes committed in order to obtain the means of procuring the drug.[1]

The British-chartered East India Company and its successors (1600–1874), exercising a controlling government-sponsored monopoly of all British-Asian trade, sold freely to Chinese merchants. The cultivation of opium in India was part of this monopoly and this, in turn, gave the East India Company virtually a world monopoly on opium.

The Chinese attempted to terminate the traffic in opium, but were defeated by the British in the Opium War of 1840–1842. This defeat resulted in the signing of the Treaty of Nanking, which opened China to free trade, and the opium traffic continued to flourish. It continued to be a major source of Indian revenue until the traffic was finally terminated on May 8, 1911. The British are not to bear all of the blame, however. Almost one-fifth of the opium entering Shanghai in 1858, for example, was carried by American ships.

Chinese immigrants to the United States also smoked opium. It was also used to relieve pain during the Civil War and was included in a variety of patent medicines developed to remedy many diseases. The use of opium (and its derivative morphine) as ingredients in patent medicines became so universal in this country by the turn of the century that the Harrison Narcotic Act of 1914 was passed to stem a rising addiction rate among United States citizens.

DRUGS AS STIMULANTS

Some two million highland inhabitants of the Peruvian Andes have used the leaves of the Erythroxylon coca plant for centuries as a source of cocaine. To release the cocaine, they annually chew or otherwise consume over nine tons of the plant's leaves. The natives claim that fatigue is forgotten, physical strength is improved, and intellectual capabilities are increased.

The use of drugs as stimulants began in a number of ways. It was Köller and Freud [2] who, in the later 1800's, noted the mental stimulant properties of cocaine while evaluating the drug's local anesthetic properties. The use of the compound as a local anesthetic grew rapidly but so did its use as a mental stimulant. Addiction to cocaine became a severe problem, with the result that cocaine also was placed under Federal

---

[1] Excerpted from G. H. Smith, "On Opium Smoking Among the Chinese," *The Lancet*. 1:707, 1841–42.

[2] Dr. Sigmund Freud, physician and founder of psychoanalysis, and Dr. Karl Köller, physician (ophthalmologist).

TABLE I

STATUTORY PENALTIES [3] FOR ILLEGAL SALE AND POSSESSION OF NARCOTICS AND RESTRICTED DANGEROUS DRUGS *

DRUG	SALE			SALE TO MINORS			POSSESSION [1]			CALIFORNIA HEALTH AND SAFETY CODE SECTION
	1st offense	2nd [2] offense	3rd offense	1st offense	2nd offense	3rd offense	1st offense	2nd offense	3rd offense	
Heroin, opium, morphine, codeine, Demerol, etc., cocaine	5 yrs. to life	10 yrs. to life	15 yrs. to life	10 yrs. to life	10 yrs. to life	15 yrs. to life	2 yrs. to 10 yrs.	5 yrs. to 20 yrs.	15 yrs. to life	11500 11501 11502 11530.5
Marijuana	5 yrs. to life	5 yrs. to life	10 yrs. to life	10 yrs. to life	10 yrs. to life	15 yrs. to life	2 yrs. to 10 yrs.	5 yrs. to 15 yrs.	10 yrs. to life	11531 11532
LSD, DMT Depressants: Nembutal, Seconal, etc. (barbiturates) Miltown, Librium (tranquilizers) Stimulants: Benzedrine (amphetamine), Methamphetamine (Desoxyn, etc.)	Jail [4] or 1 yr. to 5 yrs.	2 yrs. to 10 yrs.		1 yr. to 5 yrs.	2 yrs. to 10 yrs.		Fine or jail of maximum 1 yr.	Jail or 1 yr. to 5 yrs.		11910 11912 11913

DRUG	SALE			SALE TO MINORS			POSSESSION [1]			CALIFORNIA HEALTH AND SAFETY CODE SECTION
	1st offense	2nd [2] offense	3rd offense	1st offense	2nd offense	3rd offense	1st offense	2nd offense	3rd offense	
Other prescription drugs (antibiotics, etc.)	Fine or jail of 1 yr. maximum						Not restricted			26255, also B & P Code, Sec. 4227

[1] Many of these drugs may be sold and possessed on the prescription of a physician. However, no such exemption exists for heroin, marijuana, LSD, or DMT.

[2] Second and third offenses include other violations of narcotic laws.

[3] The law also specifies minimal times which must be served prior to parole.

[4] A misdemeanor is a fine or jail sentence not to exceed one year. Any sentence over one year is a felony.

* Source: California Health and Safety Code, 1965.

* Reprinted from *"The New Generation and the New Drugs,"* D. E. Smith, and F. M. Meyers, *California Health*, February, 1968.

control, under the previously mentioned Harrison Narcotic Act of 1914. Physicians continue to use it as a local anesthetic. Illicit use is rather limited due to the penalties imposed by the law (see Table I on pages 8–9), high cost, and the ready availability of cheaper synthetic drugs such as the amphetamines (Benzedrine ®, Methedrine ®, and others).

Peoples of the Middle East and Ethiopia used "khat" (a stimulant drug that produces effects similar to those produced by the amphetamines) many hundreds of years ago to overcome the pangs of hunger, the misery of horrible living conditions, and the fatigue of long and arduous physical labor.

Methedrine (speed, crystal) is the best known derivative of the amphetamines. It and its chemical relatives can be traced to the research of a California pharmacologist in the 1930's. He determined that the active ingredient in "khat" closely resembled the amphetamines. With his discovery as a guide, many synthetic chemicals were produced with similar actions (for example, Benzedrine ®, Methedrine ®, Dexedrine ®, and Desoxyn ®). These drugs were initially used on prescription of a physician for weight control and to overcome fatigue but now are included in the psychedelic [3] drug group and are often obtained by illegal means.

Some misuse of these compounds has occurred, particularly by persons who have obtained the drugs by prescription, as the following account illustrates:

A patient requested Dexedrine capsules for purposes of weight control. Her health otherwise had been good and she had no physical disease to contraindicate the use of the drug. I prescribed 50 capsules containing 15 mgm of Dexedrine to be taken once a day.

From that day on I found an increasing number of calls to me or my office nurse for refills of this prescription. At first such excuses of lost prescription or breakage were accepted but when her requests became more frequent, our suspicions were aroused.

It became clear that she had addicted herself to Dexedrine. I found that she was obtaining Dexedrine from other physicians and stealing from friends who used the drug. A number of telephone calls to my office by the patient, while she was strongly under the influence of Dexedrine and perhaps other drugs, convinced me of her sorry plight.[4]

---

[3] Hallucinogenic.
[4] Related to the author by a fellow physician.

SOME HALLUCINOGENIC DRUGS

Many drugs affect the human mind (see Table II on pages 12–13). Mind "expanding" compounds (hallucinogens) appear to have existed for centuries. The earliest human beings no doubt experienced anxieties and disappointments which disrupted their lives or made them unhappy, much as in our times. Perhaps some individual inadvertently discovered that chewing a certain kind of leaf or crushing or burning a particular seed produced pleasant effects on his mind and offered temporary relief from anxiety.

One of these hallucinogens, marihuana (often called hashish, "pot," or "tea") is used by millions of people. It reputedly was first described in use during the year 3 B.C. (The United Nations listed a worldwide user figure of 200 million even in 1951.) The name "marihuana" itself can be traced to Mexico, where the plant was first reported sometime in the 1600's.

Although many attempts have been made to curb its use by establishing laws, none of these attempts have been successful in those places where the drug has become a part of the culture (parts of Africa, Asia, and Latin America). The plant *Cannabis sativa,* from which marihuana is derived, is more commonly called hemp. It is found both wild and cultivated in many parts of the world. In the 1850's the hemp plant occupied an important place in our economy as a source of rope. It was recognized until 1937 by the United States Pharmacopeia as tincture of cannabis and prescribed by physicians for its medicinal effects.

The Persians were apparently well-acquainted with hashish, as the origin of the English word "assassin" shows. The word is derived from the Arabic "Hashshashin," the Order of the Assassins, founded by a Middle Eastern Moslem named Hosan-i-Sabbah some time around 1090 A.D. Agents of this "religious" Order were first intoxicated with hashish before being sent on missions of secret assassination.

The Christians who participated in the Crusades brought back tales of these Assassins, as well as descriptions of the effects that the strange (to them) compound produced in humans. The Chinese knew that marihuana could be derived from hemp, with the female hemp plant being the source of the resin that produces the drug's effects on the mind. Traders took the hemp plant from its Far Eastern origin along trade routes through the Middle East and into Europe. In many parts of India, marihuana was and is used in religious ceremonies. Concerned by the spread of the drug's use, the British established an Indian Hemp Drugs Commission which published what many consider to be a classic report on hemp in 1894. Three statements from that report are worth noting.

1. There is no evidence of any weight regarding mental and moral injuries from the <u>moderate</u> use of these drugs.

TABLE II
SOME HALLUCINOGENS USED THROUGHOUT THE WORLD *

SUBSTANCE	ACTIVE PRINCIPLE	SOURCE	MAJOR AREA OF USE	PURPOSE	HOW TAKEN
1. Glue	Toluene	Commercial	U. S. A.	Euphoria	Sniff
2. Gas vapor	Trichlorethylene, cyclohexanol, ethylene dichloride, toluene	Commercial	U. S. A.	Euphoria, hedonism	Sniff
3. Cannabis (marijuana, bhang, dagga, kif, hashish)	Cannabinol	C. sativa (C. indica)	World-wide	Pleasure	Smoke, drink, food
4. Peyote	Mescaline (epinephrine-like)	Cactus, L. williamsii	U. S. A., Mexico	Religious, ritual, hedonism	Chew, drink (can inject mescaline)
5. Psilocin, psilocybin	Serotonin derivatives	Basiodiomycete P. mexicana (teonanactyl)	Mexico, U. S. A.	Religious, ritual	Oral
6. Ololiuqui	Lysergic acid	Rivea corymbosa	Mexico	Pleasure, ritual	Chew seeds
7. Pituri	Scopolamine	Potato-like shrub Dubiosia hopwoodii	Australia	Relief from thirst, strength	Chew mixed with ashes or acacia wood

8. Caapi (Yahee) (ayahuasca)	Banisterine	Vine-Banisteria caapi	South America (Colombia, Brazil)	Whipping ceremony, aphrodisiac, prophecy	Drink
9. Datura	Stramonium scopolamine, hyoscyamine	Datura sp.	Mexico, Ecuador, Peru, Colombia	Aphrodisiac, religious, magic	Drink
10. Ibogaine	Harmine (banisterine)	Plant-iboga tabernanthe	Africa	Stimulant, ordeal ceremony	Chew
11. Fly agaric	Muscarine bufotenine	Basidiomycete A. muscaria	Siberia	Pleasure relief from environment	Drink, chew
12. Yakee epina	Myristicine, DMT, bufotenine	Virola sp. (nutmeg)	Venezuela, Brazil, Colombia	Religious, magic	Snuff
13. Vinho de Juremena	Nigarine (dimethyl-tryptamine)	Mimosa hostilis	South America	Religious, magic	Drink
14. Cohoba (yopo, niopo)	Bufotenine, DMT,	Piptadenia peregrina	Colombia Venezuela	Magic, warfare, orgiastic	Snuff
15. ———		Saliva divinarum	Mexico	Religious, magic	Chew leaves

* Reprinted from D. B. Louria, "The Abuse of LSD," in *LSD: Man and Society*, R. C. Debold and R. C. Leaf, eds., Middletown, Conn.: Wesleyan Univ. Press, 1967. Copyright © 1967 by Wesleyan Univ. Reprinted by permission Wesleyan Univ. Press and Faber & Faber.

2. Large numbers of practitioners of long experience have seen no evidence of any connections between the moderate use of hemp drugs and disease.

3. Moderation does not lead to excess in hemp any more than it does in alcohol. Regular, moderate use of ganja (a specially cultivated and harvested grade of the female plants of Indian hemp) and bhang (a decoction or a smoking mixture derived from the cut tops of uncultivated female plants in which the resin content is usually low) produces the same effects as moderate and regular doses of whiskey. Excess is confined to the idle and dissipated.[5]

A similar feeling was expressed in a report issued by the New York Academy of Medicine as part of the LaGuardia Report in 1944.[6] That the present stir over marihuana usage is by no means new is shown by the reaction of Mr. Harry Anslinger, former United States Commissioner of Narcotics, to the 1944 report. He wrote that "the [Narcotics] Bureau immediately detected the superficiality and hollowness of its findings and denounced it."

In 1937, the Marihuana Tax Act was passed by the United States Federal Government. It placed the same type of controls over marihuana as the Harrison Narcotic Act of 1914 placed over the narcotic drugs. Until recently the impact of such legislation was of little concern to the majority of the people in this country. At present a lively debate rages about the degree of control needed for this *non*addictive drug. Penalties for use of marihuana are comparable to those for addictive drugs like heroin, use being considered a felony.

Another mind-expanding drug was discovered among the Indians of the Southwest United States, who have used the cactus plant as part of their religious ceremonies for 150 to 200 years. Mescaline is an active ingredient derived from the cactus, and its effects play an important part in the lives of these Indian tribes. *Peyote* is the Indian word for both the religious ceremony and the strange cactus button that is an important part of their ritual. The following is an account of the experiences of Alice Marriott, a white person, who was a participant in a healing ceremony conducted by a Cheyenne Tribe in the early 1950's:

An ordinary brown paper bag was passed containing the peyote beads or pods. To Alice they looked like a walnut, shrivelled, greyish green or greyish brown in color with tufts of white fuzz. . . . Each

---

[5] Report of the Indian Hemp Drugs Commission, 1893–94.
[6] *New York City, Mayor's Committee on Marihuana: The Marihuana Problem in the City of New York; Sociological, Medical, Psychological and Pharmacological Studies,* Lancaster, Pa.: Jacques Cattell Press, 1944.

participant in the teepee took a peyote button. . . . In all, four buttons were eaten during the first part of the night. . . . After swallowing the last peyote she suddenly saw a change in the fire. Colors she had not imagined appeared, whirled, turned and blended, mixing and separating. "They revolved before me in a wheel of richness and brilliance."

She no longer heard words. Only light, color, and beauty was apparent. She felt cool in a delightful way. . . . "It was like paradise." [7]

LSD

The source of the chemical LSD (lysergic acid diethylamide) is the rye fungus, ergot. LSD was first synthesized in 1938 as a chemical precursor to some other ergot compounds. The remarkable mental effects it is capable of producing were not appreciated until 1943 when Dr. Albert Hofmann, working at the Sandoz Laboratories in Switzerland, accidentally ingested some of the compound. He describes the resulting effects as follows:

In the afternoon of April 16, 1943, when I was working on this problem, I was seized by a peculiar sensation of vertigo and restlessness. Objects, as well as the shape of my associates in the laboratory, appeared to undergo optical changes. I was unable to concentrate on my work. In a dream-like state I left for home, where an irresistible urge to lie down overcame me. I drew the curtains and immediately fell into a peculiar state similar to a drunkenness, characterized by an exaggerated imagination. With my eyes closed, fantastic pictures of extraordinary plasticity and intensive color seemed to surge toward me. After two hours this state gradually wore off.[8]

The experience of Hofmann and several others led some people to believe that an LSD experience represented a kind of model psychosis.[9] It was believed, therefore, that LSD might be used as a means by which to study psychoses. This thinking appeared to have largely been proven erroneous in the later 1950's, but by this time popular use of the drug began to grow.

The Doors of Perception, written by Aldous Huxley in 1957, explored the mind-expanding powers of mescaline as experienced by the

---

[7] Excerpted from Charlotte M. Cardon, "Peyote and the Native American Church," *Journal of Psychedelic Drugs,* 1:73–76, 1967.
[8] Excerpted from A. Hofmann, "Psychotomimetic Drugs: Chemical and Pharmacological Aspects," *Acta Physiol. & Pharmac.* Neer 8:244–246, 1959.
[9] A psychosis is a serious form of mental disease. A model psychosis would provide an example of typical psychotic symptoms.

author. (Mescaline has effects very similar to those of LSD.) The "psy-chedelic cult" of Professors Timothy Leary and Richard Alpert at Harvard University developed shortly afterwards, and the modern LSD era began. The news media helped to spread the story of LSD and contributed to the result that today it and related chemicals are in widespread use. LSD is considered, from a medical standpoint, as an investigational drug whose safety or effectiveness has not been established.

The use of drugs continues today both legally and illegally. The use of stimulant drugs such as Methedrine has increased in the past years some five to six-fold. The number of persons addicted to narcotics (opium, morphine, heroin, and various synthetic drugs) is estimated at about 200,000 in the United States. (Table I indicates the penalties associated with illegal use.) Though many differences exist among the psychedelic drugs, there seems to be little question that people are using them in increasing number and that this use seems destined to continue.

What Do You Think?

1. Drug use, it seems, is hardly new. Why then does there seem to be so much attention paid to the problem during the last decade? Drugs have been in use for centuries. Why should the fact be recognized so suddenly and so forcefully just now?

2. Some writers have indicated that in the future drugs may well be the answer to many social problems. Aldous Huxley's *Brave New World* implies this. Yet Huxley seems to object to the use of drugs in managing a massive society of tremendous proportion and wants. Might drug use become widespread as a means by which to attain personal and social satisfaction? Might drugs be used to "manage" an entire society? Would such a society be able to function effectively?

Today's Drug Scene: What Is It?

How widespread is the use of drugs? Who uses them? What is a "drug trip" like? What effects do drugs produce? The large number of drugs and the misuse of terms describing drugs that alter mood and behavior have introduced a great deal of confusion. It may be helpful, therefore, to start this chapter with a few definitions:

As has been shown, a "drug" is a chemical substance that alters mood, perception, or consciousness. It is to be emphasized that the place of drugs has not been definitely and finally established in our society. The field of psychiatry has long employed drugs in treatment, with significantly beneficial results. There is also evidence of significantly detrimental aspects to drug usage. The following may help define the problem.

Drug abuse: A general term implying that a person habitually takes a drug that is unacceptable to the society in which the person lives.

Addiction: A frequently misused term that means different things to different people. We will consider it equivalent in meaning to the term drug abuse.

Psychological dependence (habituation): A pattern of drug use developed by persons who repeatedly self-administer drugs and who eventually come to feel that they cannot carry on normal everyday activities unless they take drugs.

Physical dependence: A condition that may accompany the chronic and excessive use of a drug. If a person takes large amounts of drugs on a regular basis, certain alterations of his normal body functions occur which when the drug is withdrawn or stopped may lead to serious illness. This illness or disease is called the withdrawal or abstinence

17

syndrome and is seen with such drugs as heroin, morphine, Demerol, Methedrine, Dexedrine, and the barbiturates.

Tolerance: The necessity for taking higher and higher doses of a drug in order to get a desired effect. This is why many drug users have to continually increase their intake of a drug.

Many of the readings which follow refer to drug use in general. When particular drugs are being considered, they will be specifically indicated as such. As you read, however, you should continually ask yourself: Is what is being said true of *all* drugs, or does it depend on the particular *kind* of drug being considered? The readings which follow provide some brief thoughts and viewpoints on the drug scene for you to consider.

1.   "A NEW PHENOMENON HAS BURST UPON THE AMERICAN SCENE"

A juvenile court judge succinctly describes the recent emergence of drugs in California. Would this be true of your state?

Like a volcanic eruption, a new phenomenon has burst upon the American scene—the use of drugs and narcotics by our youth. San Mateo County (California) is typical of this explosion. In the ten years between 1956 and 1965 inclusive, there was a total of 45 drug referrals to the juvenile court. In 1966, the single year's total of such referrals was 157, and in the first six months of 1967, it had mushroomed to 202.[1]

A student poll taken in a California high school population showed almost 60 per cent of the students had used marihuana on at least one occasion. Over 40 per cent admitted to a continuing and chronic use.

A 1967 San Mateo County (California) health report indicated that 14 per cent of that county's senior high school students used LSD on a regular basis and gave the following picture of the teen-age drug user:

The composite picture of the boy drug user in the school setting is a youngster with at least average and probably above average ability who is usually earning "C's and D's," who truants at least occasionally, but who is not a severe discipline problem. The drug-using girls are likely to be of above average intelligence earning "C" grades, attending school with reasonable regularity and not considered a discipline problem. . . .

---

[1] Excerpted from the *Narcotics Inquiry Report,* San Mateo County (California) Juvenile Justice Commission, November 1967.

It is clear that illegal drug users do not fit a stereotype and are not so unique as to warrant special and unusual probation programs.[2]

In a poll conducted by the American Institute of Public Opinion for the *Reader's Digest* magazine, young men and women college student representing some 426 American colleges reported:

Not more than 6 per cent of the students polled had even tried marihuana, including those who had taken only a few puffs at a party or on a dare. Not more than 1 per cent had experimented with LSD. The students interviewed thought that about 13 per cent of their fellow students nationwide used drugs; but when queried about the situation on their own campuses the average dropped abruptly to 4 per cent. Fifty-one per cent said that they did not know a single student who had puffed a joint or embarked on a psychedelic LSD trip.[3]

A study of drug use among California teen-agers involved 9,000 students in 20 cities. It took a year to complete and was conducted by Dr. Joel Fort, a psychiatrist especially concerned about the drug problem. Consider the following figures:

1. In the 12th grade 42 per cent of all students had smoked pot while more than 85 per cent of all students had used alcohol.
2. In the 7th grade 37 per cent of the boys and 32 per cent of the girls had smoked pot.
3. 6–11 per cent of students (grades 7–12) have tried LSD.
4. 3–5 per cent of students (grades 7–12) have used heroin although the study found no heroin addicts in the group questioned.
5. In the 12th grade at least 15 per cent have used amphetamines.
6. The socio-economic background and ethnic group of the students did not appear to influence drug use.[4]

What Do You Think?

1. How does the evidence presented in these studies compare with drug use in your locality? On what information did you base your comparison?

---

[2] Excerpted from the *Narcotics Inquiry Report,* San Mateo County (California) Juvenile Justice Commission, November 1967.
[3] Excerpted from Fred Dickenson, "Drugs on Campus: A Gallup Poll," *The Reader's Digest,* November, 1967.
[4] Excerpted from Don Wegars, "Pot vs. Alcohol Among The Teens," *San Francisco Chronicle,* December 11, 1968.

2.   The statistics presented appear to conflict. How would you explain this?

2.   A MISSIONARY ZEAL *

The Medical Director of the Haight-Ashbury Clinic and consultant on drug abuse to the San Francisco General Hospital presents a brief description of the "hippie" community's use of drugs.

They (the hippies) live communally. The numbers of them who can find shelter in a single room is remarkable. They tend strongly towards mysticism and asceticism.[1] Association with asceticism is a form of infantilism. This may show itself not only in barefootedness and childish diets. In grocery stores in the neighborhood the hippies may be seen spending their few coins on soda pop, popsicles, candy bars, and starches. Emaciation is commonplace, malnutrition is endemic, finally use of drugs is taken as an article of faith, consciously, assertively, sometimes almost with missionary zeal. Certainly among those hippies who reach the clinic as patients, use of drugs is consistently a major factor in morbidity.[2] . . .

They're (approximate population of Haight-Ashbury in the summer of 1967 was 20,000) salvageable kids taking large quantities of drugs based on a philosophic rationale. And they'd rather be sick than abandon it. . . .

Venereal disease is epidemic. . . .

Communal use of needle for drug injection leads to an incidence of serum hepatitis which is abnormally high when compared to a similar group not engaged in regular drug use and not living in the Haight-Ashbury.

What Do You Think?

What does the author mean when he says that use of drugs among the hippies is "taken as an article of faith"? What factors might produce this?

---

* Excerpted from "Hippie Health Clinic," *Roche Medical Image* Hoffman-LaRoche and Company, Nutley, New Jersey, 1967. Courtesy Roche Laboratories and *Roche Medical Image*.
[1] Self-denial of customary wants in pursuit of spiritual goals.
[2] Disease.

3. "ALMOST ANYBODY CAN GET IT FOR YOU " *

What are the sources of drugs? How easily can they be obtained? From whom? The following information as to the availability and use of drugs was compiled at a youth meeting held at a high school in 1967.

The general consensus was that any and all drugs were "readily available" and that "almost anybody can get it for you."

Almost everyone knew of someone at the high school level who uses drugs but the sources vary. Some felt that high school students or young adults in their 20's who had the mobility might provide drugs to a high school contact. Some students went up to the city (San Francisco) to the Haight-Ashbury and brought drugs back to the high schools. "We know the friends who get it from someone we may or may not know." The profit motive seemed not to be important "when you were dealing with your friends" but all felt that somewhere along the line, usually at the ultimate source, someone was making a profit. The cost of drugs depended on whom you were buying it from. A matchbox of marihuana, for example, cost from $3 to $5. A "lid" ranged from $7.00 to $15, though averaging about $10.00. A kilo or kilogram ranged from $75.00 to $90.00. The cost of LSD, though variable, was estimated at $3.00 per cap and $4.00 for a tab (you were lucky if in a cap you got 100 micrograms of LSD). A number of students did not know what "speed" was but one "authority" stated that for $3.00 you could buy enough "speed" (Methedrine) or amphetamine usually to give you four or five "trips." The prices of most other drugs were unknown to the youngsters.

Without question the most commonly used drug was marihuana, with LSD second and speed or the amphetamines considered the most likely candidate for third. Some students put prescription pills (like No-Doz or Dexedrine) as number three along with speed. One youngster considered sedatives as number four and almost all agreed that when glue was used, it was sniffed predominantly by youngsters below the 8th grade but that they themselves had little or no use for it. All denied using heroin.

---

* Excerpted from the *Narcotics Inquiry Report,* San Mateo County (California) Juvenile Justice Commission, November, 1967.

What Do You Think?

> This article suggests that drugs are "readily available." Would this be true in your community? How can such ready availability be diminished?

4. THE SOURCE OF DRUGS

From where are drugs obtained? The next reading suggests some sources of supply:

LSD in the Tenderloin (in San Francisco) is almost exclusively a homemade product as LSD is no longer available from legitimate sources. . . . .

Methedrine (crystal, crink, speed) used in the Tenderloin comes in liquid, tablet, capsule and powder form. It is legitimately manufactured and reaches the market in the same manner as pills. This drug can also be made at home by persons with the essential lab techniques and equipment.[1]

LSD is even harder to control and if you look at the control situation, that boils down to who controls the raw material—lysergic acid. . . . It turns out that many of the people who sell LSD do so because they believe it is of social significance, and while they take out enough to live usually they don't milk the market for all it is worth. That is probably why the syndicate—or the Mafia, or whatever you want to call it—hasn't gotten into LSD in a big way because there are so many people who are willing to sell it and because they believe in it. In a way it is usually passed from human contact to human contact and your connection is usually somebody you know, rather than somebody you meet on a street corner, although that is something that certainly does happen quite often.[2]

A pusher can be anyone from a teen-ager to a housewife. The pusher will sometimes cut (weaken) the drug with any one of a number of substances. Doing this increases his volume and likewise his profits. The pusher sometimes also may be a user who is pushing to support his own habit. The pusher and his supplier maintain close contact in order

---

[1] Excerpted from *Drugs in the Tenderloin,* Central City Multi-Service Center, 272 Sixth Street, San Francisco, California, 1967.
[2] Excerpted from R. Alpert, "A Symposium: Psychedelic Drugs and the Law," *Journal of Psychedelic Drugs,* Vol. 1, 1967.

to coordinate drug shipments, payments and reactions to police activity. The pusher's understanding of drug laws is almost nil. Many believe, for example, that the possession of marihuana, a relatively harmless substance, would be a less serious crime than possession of Methedrine, a substantially more dangerous drug, while in practice, of course, the reverse is true. . . .

The Tenderloin drug market is a loosely structured operation. Contrary to some popular opinion, there is not an organized "syndicate" drug operation in the Tenderloin.

However there is an organized "syndicate" operation involving bars, restaurants and night clubs. The "syndicate" has an interest in keeping the Tenderloin drug market in operation in order to provide a climate where "syndicate" operations can flourish. The thousands of dollars a month poured into the Tenderloin drug market by the "syndicate" do not produce a profit for the "syndicate" but do help to keep police activity directed away from other "syndicate" activities. Very few suppliers and pushers in the Tenderloin know of the "syndicate" involvement in the Tenderloin drug market.

The pills, barbiturates, Dexedrine, Benzedrine, etc. sold in the Tenderloin market usually come from diversion from pharmaceutical companies. The pills are smuggled out by employees or may be obtained from profiteering doctors or pharmacists. Occasionally a pharmacy is burglarized and a flood of pills hits the market.

Marihuana: The marihuana smoked in the Tenderloin comes from Mexico and is usually transported into this country in the form of "kilos" (2.2 lb. compressed bricks of marihuana). It is brought through customs concealed in various objects such as dolls, clothing or hidden in automobiles.

Heroin: Most of the heroin in the Tenderloin comes from Mexico. It is either smuggled into the country in the same manner as marihuana or because of the small size of the packages concealed within an individual's body.[3]

What Do You Think?

1.   The author states that many people sell LSD because they "believe in it." What do you think this means?

2.   Can drug sources such as the ones described in this reading be eliminated? Why or why not?

---

[3] Excerpted from *Drugs in the Tenderloin,* Central City Multi-Service Center, 272 Sixth Street, San Francisco, California, 1967.

5.   THE USE OF MARIHUANA *

The smoking of marihuana, or "pot," is by no means new, as we have seen. Here is a description of what one individual experienced in the 1850's.

One morning, in the spring of 185–, I dropped in upon the doctor for my accustomed visit. "Have you seen," said he, "my new acquisitions?"

I looked toward the shelves in the direction of which he pointed, and saw, added since my last visit, a row of comely pasteboard cylinders inclosing vials of various extracts. Arranged in order according to their size, they confronted me, as pretty a little rank of medicinal sharpshooters as could gratify the eye of an amateur. I approached the shelves, that I might take them in review.

A rapid glance showed most of them to be old acquaintances. "Conium, taraxacum, rhubarb—ha!! what is this? Cannabis indica?" "That," answered the doctor, looking with a parental fondness upon his new treasure, "is a preparation of the East Indian hemp, a powerful agent in case of lock-jaw." On the strength of this introduction, I took down the little archer [container]. To pull out a broad and shallow cork was the work of an instant, and it revealed to me an olive-brown extract, of the consistency of pitch, and a decided aromatic odor. . . . I waited till my friend was out of sight, that I might not terrify him by that which he considered a suicidal venture, and removed from his store of offensive armor a pill. This, I swallowed without a tremor as to the danger of the result. Making all due allowance for the fact that I had not taken the hasheesh bolus fasting, I ought to experience its effects within the next four hours. That time elapsed without bringing the shadow of a phenomenon. It was plain that my dose had been insufficient.

For the sake of observing the most conservative prudence, I suffered several days to go by without a repetition of the experiment, and then, keeping the matter equally secret, I administered to myself a pill of fifteen grains. This second was equally ineffectual with the first.

Gradually, by five grains at a time, I increased the dose to thirty grains, which I took one evening half an hour after tea. I had now almost come to the conclusion that I was absolutely unsusceptible of the hasheesh influence. Without any expectation that this last experiment would be

---

* Excerpted from "Selections from the Hashish Eater," by Fitzbergh Ludlow in *The Marihuana Papers,* David Solomon, ed. Indianapolis, Indiana: The Bobbs-Merrill Company, Inc., 1966.

more successful than the former ones, and indeed with no realization of the manner in which the drug affected those who did make the experiment successfully, I went to pass the evening at the house of an intimate friend. In music and conversation the time passed pleasantly. The clock struck ten, reminding me that three hours had elapsed since the dose was taken, and as yet not an unusual symptom had appeared. I was provoked to think that this trial was as fruitless as its predecessors.

Ha! what means this sudden thrill? A shock, as of some unimagined vital force, shoots without warning through my entire frame, leaping to my fingers' ends, piercing my brain, startling me till I almost spring from my chair.

I could not doubt it. I was in the power of the hasheesh influence. My first emotion was one of uncontrollable terror—a sense of getting something which I had not bargained for. That moment I would have given all I had or hoped to have to be as I was three hours before.

No pain anywhere—not a twinge in any fibre—yet a cloud of unutterable strangeness was settling upon me, and wrapping me impenetrably in from all that was natural or familiar. Endeared faces, well known to me of old, surrounded me, yet they were not with me in my loneliness. I had entered upon a tremendous life which they could not share. . . . A nearness of place, with an infinite distance of state, a connection which had no possible sympathies for the wants of that hour of revelation, an isolation none the less perfect for seeming companionship.

Still I spoke; a question was put to me, and I answered it; I even laughed at a bon mot. Yet it was not my voice which spoke; perhaps one which I once had far away in another time and another place. For a while I knew nothing that was going on externally, and then the remembrance of the last remark which had been made returned slowly and indistinctly, as some trait of a dream will return after many days, puzzling as to say where we have been conscious of it before.

A fitful wind all the evening had been sighing down the chimney; it now grew into the steady hum of a vast wheel in accelerating motion. For a while this hum seemed to resound through all space. I was stunned by it. Slowly the revolution of the wheel came to a stop, and its monotonous din was changed for the reverberating peal of a grand cathedral organ. The ebb and flow of its inconceivably solemn tone filled me with a grief that was more than human. I sympathized with the dirge-like cadence as spirit sympathizes with spirit. And then, in the full conviction that all I heard and felt was real, I looked out of my isolation to see the effect of the music on my friends. Ah! we were in separate worlds indeed. Not a trace of appreciation on any face.

What Do You Think?

1.   How would you describe the author's experience?
2.   What does he mean when he says at the end of the article "Ah! we were in separate worlds indeed."?

6.   "IT IS LIKE SEEING THE DOOR TO LIFE SWING OPEN " *

Next is the description of an Indian ceremony among the Cheyenne in which a white woman swallowed peyote. Compare the description of her experience with that of the author in Reading 5.

Alice Marriott had long been interested in Indian culture and had won the friendship of an Indian woman named Mary. This friendship and a lingering illness led Alice to consider becoming the object of a Cheyenne healing ceremony. The ceremony was to be conducted by Mary's uncle.

In deference to her white friend's poor health Mary finally agreed that Alice needed help. The date of the ceremony was arranged. She told Alice that when her uncle "heals with peyote" he asks the sick person to contribute the food for dinner on the day after the ceremony and to provide tobacco and the peyote, as well as other needs for the ceremony. "But you are like his own child and he will put up the teepee and give you the whole ceremony—which is a great event for those who believe."

It would be a social occasion too, with pies to be baked, a big steer roasted outdoors with barbecue sauce, salads and hot coffee. Not everyone who came to the tribe would take part in the healing but many would stay for a social visit.

The event was scheduled for Saturday night and on Friday Miss Marriott was forbidden to eat salt because "peyote doesn't like salt." She was then taken by one of the women, (not Mary) to a lodge for a series of steam baths which proved very weakening. But she was assured that now she was clean and could go through the rites purified of external grime and dust.

Fasting was done all day Saturday and Alice rested, feeling exhausted and very, very hot—perhaps with a slight recurrence of an earlier fever. After 4 P.M. she was permitted no more water with the warning if she cheated she would become sick during the ceremony.

---

* Excerpted from Charlotte M. Cardon, "Peyote and the Native American Church," *Journal of Psychedelic Drugs,* 1:73–76, 1967.

One of the women, who would stay with her during the night in the teepee, dressed her in a straight, cotton print dress with kimono sleeves, an overskirt, shawl and moccasins. Her hair was short so she wore the shawl over her head going into the teepee.

It was a large canvas teepee rising sheer and white against the darkening sky of dusk. The temperature was still hovering around 100 degrees but the men who would take part in the ritual were dressed splendidly in buckskins and boots with fur turbans. Mary's uncle as chief, wore a magnificent wool blanket of blue and scarlet and fanned himself with an eagle-feather fan although he seemed otherwise oblivious to the heat of day.

A foot or so inside the canvas wall a curving bed of wild sage had been laid and blankets spread on it. A small fire burned in the center but the vast room was cool. About 30 people entered the teepee—both men and women. Members of the Cheyenne tribe came to do special honor to Miss Marriott.

On the ground before each person were small mounds of oak leaves. The edges were folded and stuffed with tobacco for making cigarettes. Each individual folded his own. A cedar stick was passed like incense to light up the first smoke.

In a high voice the uncle began a chant and welcomed his guests as a host. "Relax and have a good time" he reminded his group. A drum made of a three-legged iron kettle covered with buckskin was beaten to accompany the opening song and a gourd rattle was shaken until the song had been repeated four times—seemingly a mystic number.

Then an ordinary brown paper bag was passed containing the peyote beads or pods. To Alice they looked like a walnut, shrivelled, greyish green or greyish brown in color with tufts of white fuzz.

Her female companion sat with hands crossed in lap, palms upward with the peyote lying in the right palm. Each participant in the teepee took a peyote button and rolled four cigarettes. The pod was elevated toward the fire and withdrawn to the heart three times. Then with great reverence the old Indian leader placed it in his mouth and chewed the pulp.

Dried peyote puckers the mouth and tongue and dries the mucous lining of the mouth. Thoroughly dried, it swells and almost chokes the individual. It seemed to have an indescribable rank, green cactus taste.

The Indian next to Miss Marriott spit out the chewed button, rolled it into a ball and tossed the wad back into her mouth and swallowed it. Then a cigarette was lighted which gave relief to the scratching unpleasant pain in the throat. Alice found she could follow suit. In all, four buttons were eaten during the first part of the night.

"Nothing out of the ordinary happened," Miss Marriott remembers, "except each button was less unpleasant to take than the one before."

After several hours a lull occurred and at midnight a ceremonial bucket of water was blessed and passed. Only four swallows were permitted but again the cool water soothed the feeling of a scratched throat.

And then a strange event began. One of the Cheyenne Indians came up to Miss Marriott and offered her fresh green peyote. As a blood sister she should take it and it would entitle her to be a true member of the Indian tribe.

After swallowing the last peyote she suddenly saw a change in the fire. Colors she had not imagined appeared, whirled, turned and blended, mixing and separating. "They revolved before me in a wheel of richness and brilliance."

She no longer heard words. Only light, color and beauty was apparent. She felt cool in a delightful way. "The door to the teepee represented an entrance to beauty beyond the senses and beyond earth," she recalled.

Going outdoors the stars were in arcs of color and the plain was cool and calm. For several hours everyone remained around the fire slightly dozing and in dreams of a past glory. Slowly an awareness of the world returned and the men sang the dawn song in unison. Each now held a fan of many colors and the colors fluttered like visions.

More water was brought as well as parched corn, dried meat and fruit. They all ate and drank sparingly but the food was good.

Then the men sang the going-away song and Alice Marriott and her Indian friend went outdoors in the early light. She felt as if floating as after a heavy dose of quinine but with it she faced a new day feeling strong, full of life and health once more.

"It was like paradise." Once again in her own bed she fell into a sound sleep. Later at the barbecue she ate enormously of beef, potatoes, pie and more beef as the entire tribe shared the massive pot-luck picnic.

The drought and heat broke soon afterward but the peyote had strengthened and helped her. The tremendous first exhilaration lasted for several days but there was no sudden drop following it.

Mary filled with questions begged her for a description but Alice Marriott like many of the other Indians had no objective answer.

"It is like seeing the door to life swing open" she happily repeated. Mary was puzzled but it was agreed they both should leave it at that— an experience beyond words and unforgettable.

What Do You Think?

Compare Alice's description of her experience with that of the author in Reading 5. In what ways are the reports similar? Different? How would you explain these similarities and differences?

7.   OPIUM AND ITS EFFECTS *

Next a description of the effects of smoking opium among the Chinese prior to the 20th Century.

Benares opium is that chiefly used by the farmer for the preparation of "chandoo" (the composition smoked), on account of its weight and cheapness; but the consumers prefer the Patna opium, because it has a finer flavour, is stronger, and its effects more lasting.

In Penang, the opium-smokers are the Chinese, the Malays, and a very few of other nations, chiefly the native Portuguese. It is calculated that 10 per cent of the Chinese, 2½ per cent of the Malays, and about 1 per cent of other natives, are addicted to the vice of opium-smoking. The poorer classes smoke in the shops erected for that purpose, but the wealthier orders smoke privately in their own houses. The practice is almost entirely confined to the male sex, a few abandoned prostitutes of the other sex partaking of the vice. A young beginner will not be able to smoke more than five or six grains (approximately 1/75 oz.) of chandoo, while the old practitioners will consume 290 grains (approximately ⅔ oz.) daily!

The causes which lead to this dreadful habit among the Chinese are,—First, their remarkably social and luxurious disposition. In China, every person in easy circumstances has a saloon in his house, elegantly fitted up, to receive his friends, with pipes, chandoo, &c. All are invited to smoke, and many are thus induced to commence the practice from curiosity or politeness, though few of them are ever able to discontinue the vice afterwards.

Parents are in the habit of granting this indulgence to their children, apparently to prevent them from running into other vices [which are] still more detestable. . . . In painful or incurable diseases, in all kinds of mental or corporeal sufferings, in mercantile misfortunes, and in other reverses of fortune, the opium-shop is resorted to as an asylum, where, for a time at least, the unfortunate may drown the recollection of his cares and troubles in an indescribably pleasurable feeling of indifference to all around. The Malays are confident that opium-smoking inspires them with preternatural courage and bodily strength; it is, therefore, resorted to whenever any desperate act is in contemplation.

The smoking-shops are the most miserable and wretched places

---

* Excerpted from G. H. Smith, "On Opium Smoking Among the Chinese," *The Lancet.* 1:707, 1841–42. 7 Adam Street, Adelphi, London. Reprinted by permission.

imaginable: they are kept open from six in the morning till ten o'clock at night, each being furnished with from four to eight bedsteads, constructed of bamboo-spars, and covered with dirty mats and rattans. At the head of each there is placed a narrow wooden stool, which serves as a pillow or bolster; and in the centre of each shop there is a small lamp, which, while serving to light the pipes, diffuses a cheerless light through the gloomy abode of vice and misery. . . .

First, one of the pair takes up a piece of chandoo on the point of a short iron needle, and lighting it at the lamp, applies it to the small aperture (resembling the touchhole of a gun), in the head of the pipe. After a few whiffs he hands the pipe to his friend, who lights another piece of chandoo at the lamp; and thus they go on alternately smoking till they have had sufficient, or until they are unable to purchase any more of the intoxicating drug. The fume is always expelled through the nose, and old stagers even draw it into their lungs before it is expired.

During this time, they are at first loquacious, and the conversation highly animated; but, as the opium takes effect, the conversation droops, and they frequently burst out into loud laughter, from the most trifling causes, or without any apparent cause at all, unless it be from the train of thoughts passing through their excited imaginations. The next phase presents a vacancy of countenance, with pallor, and shrinking of the features, so that they resemble people convalescing from a fever. A dead silence precedes a deep sleep, which continues from half an hour to three or four hours. In this state the pulse becomes much slower, softer, and smaller than before the debauch. Such is the general process almost invariably observed among the Chinese; but with the Malays it is often very different. Instead of the placidity that ushers in the profound sleep, the Malays frequently become outrageously violent and quarrelsome, and lives are occasionally lost in these frightful orgies!

When a person has once contracted the habit of opium-smoking, he finds it extremely difficult to discontinue the vice; yet there are many instances of its being conquered by resolution of mind. In such attempts it is most dangerous to approach the opium-shops, as the smell of the chandoo produces an irresistible desire to indulge once more in the pernicious habit: neither can opium-smoking be suddenly abandoned without some substitute, as the most serious or even fatal consequences would ensue. . . .

By a continuance in this destructive practice, the physical constitution and the moral character of the individual are deteriorated or destroyed, especially among the lower classes, who are impelled to the commission of crimes, in order to obtain the means of indulging in their dominant vice.

The hospitals and poor-houses are chiefly filled with opium-smokers. In one that I had charge of the inmates averaged sixty daily, five-sixths of whom were smokers of chandoo. The baneful effects of this habit on the human constitution are conspicuously displayed by stupor, forgetfulness, general deterioration of all the mental faculties, emaciation, debility, sallow complexion, lividity of lips and eyelids, languor and lack-lustre of eye, appetite either destroyed or depraved, sweetmeats or sugar-cane being the articles that are most relished. In the morning these creatures have a most wretched appearance, evincing no symptoms of being refreshed or invigorated by sleep, however profound. There is a remarkable dryness or burning in the throat, which urges them to repeat the opium-smoking. If the dose be not taken at the usual time, there is great prostration, vertigo, torpor, discharge of water from the eyes, . . . (withdrawal syndrome). . . .

It is generally remarked, as might, a priori,[1] be expected, that the offspring of opium-smokers are weak, stunted, and decrepit. It does not appear, however, that the Chinese, in easy circumstances, and who have the comforts of life about them, are materially affected, in respect to longevity, by the private addiction to this vice, so destructive to those who live in poverty and distress. There are many persons within the sphere of my own observation, who have attained the age of sixty, seventy, and more, and who are well known as habitual opium-smokers for more than thirty years past. . . .

What Do You Think?

1. What factors would encourage a person to smoke opium?
2. Compare the experiences described in this reading with those in Readings 5 & 6. What similarities and differences do you notice? How would you explain these similarities and differences?

8. SOME USERS DESCRIBE THEIR EXPERIENCES *

What does it feel like to use drugs? A few experiences were reported in previous readings. Here are some additional accounts.

[A female Methedrine user:]
It fills you inside like this churning cloud of light with sparks shooting

---

[1] Characterizing reasoning which assumes certain things as being established earlier or already in existence.
* Excerpted from A. Hofmann, "Psychotomimetic Drugs: Chemical and Pharmacological Aspects," *Acta Physiol. & Pharmac.* 8:224–245, 1959.

off, jagged, in all the colors of the rainbow, the universe in the process of creation, and you're a part of it.

[An LSD user:]

A description of the high is superfluous, no, it is impossible. To watch a person age before your eyes, to see the bark of a tree come alive and flow across the ground, to listen to favorite music and taste and see it, these are the things that happen.

Sometimes you go way into yourself, reliving experiences from your past as if they were today. Horrible monsters fly out to scare you, then become flowers. Things change, your mind fills with colors and shapes.

Rarely you pass beyond all this to reach the place of oneness, where all is one, you are one, and great peace and truth descend. Things you have never liked, like yourself, are lovable. Thoughts you have been afraid to face, like growing old and wrinkled and dying become not only acceptable, but also a part of your fulfillment, your part in the wholeness of nature's cycle.

[A medical doctor who inadvertently discovered the effects of LSD when he swallowed some of the drug while working in his laboratory:]

I lost all count of time. . . . Space and time became more and more disorganized, and I was overcome with fears that I was going out of my mind. The worst part of it was that I was clearly aware of my condition, though I was not able to stop it. Occasionally I felt as if I was outside of my body. I thought I had died. My "ego" was suspended somewhere in space, and I saw my body lying dead on the sofa. Visual disturbances, everything appearing in impossible colour, objects out of proportion, at times the floor seemed to bend and the walls to undulate.[1] The faces of persons present changed into colourful grimaces.

What Do You Think?

    1.   Would you consider experiences like these profitable ones? Why or why not?

    2.   Suppose you were asked to respond to each of these individuals. What would you say? Explain.

9.   1000 "SPEED" ADDICTS IN THE BAY AREA? *

All drug experiences are not as elevating as some of the previous readings suggest, however. Officials of the Haight-Ashbury Medical

---

[1] Move with a wave-like motion.

* Excerpted from Donovan Bess, "San Francisco's New Drug Problem: The Shift to Speed," *San Francisco Chronicle,* August 12, 1968.

Clinic in San Francisco speak about the impact of Methedrine abuse in the Haight-Ashbury District and the San Francisco Bay Area.

The rate of amphetamine addiction here [San Francisco] has increased four-fold in the past five months, according to Dr. Ernest Dernburg, chief psychiatrist for the Haight-Ashbury Medical Clinic.

"This now is the most major drug problem in San Francisco," he said yesterday—and warned that in his view such addiction was worse than heroin addiction "because it is more insidious."

Dernburg estimated there are now about 1000 full-blown "speed" (amphetamine) addicts in the Bay Area.

The black-market use of speed has created a social illness that is spreading throughout the Bay Area, said Roger Smith, a University of California criminologist who heads an amphetamine research project sponsored by the struggling Haight-Ashbury Clinic.

"This year," said Smith, "we have many very disturbed kids here, plus older, more hostile kids and some AWOL from military services. They're randomly searching for kicks.

"They're coming in from all areas—like Orinda, Burlingame and Mill Valley—to score (purchase) speed.

"Lots of kids are going down the drain, and I'm talking about 13- and 14-year-olds.

"But the institutions that are supposed to be dealing with these problems are not doing so."

"The group that used to get out of school and go to Fort Lauderdale to drink beer now has some experience with oral amphetamines in high school or college and they are coming out to the Haight-Ashbury to 'shoot speed' (inject themselves with it)," said Dr. David Smith, the Clinic Director.

The "speed freaks," said Dr. Dernburg, swallow or inject huge doses of an amphetamine, sometimes as much as 4000 milligrams a dose. That is nearly 300 times the dose a physician may give a housewife using the drug for weight reduction.

"It's like racing one's human engine at high speeds for long periods," Dr. Dernburg said.

The user goes without sleep, sometimes for a week. He eats poorly and talks and moves physically a great deal.

"His judgment is badly affected after a period of high doses," he said. "He is physically combative, assaultive and frequently the suspicious aspects of his personality dominate." The victims have horrible experiences.

When a user "overamps" (gets a peak jolt of the drug), said "Crystal" a 23-year-old woman veteran of speed, his "head falls off and bounces along the floor."

"You get hallucinations after using it for awhile," said Chuck, 20, who got his first "needle" years ago. "I began to think I was covered with little bugs. The shimmer of light on the hairs on my arm were bugs, so I took showers a lot and used an antiseptic to try to get them off.

"When you're this way you think people you know are cops."

"I was in agony," said "Crystal." "I was having nightmares while still awake. They still come back."

"Crystal" said she quit speed two months ago after a "friend" gave her two doses of a drug which made her limbs swell up badly and sent her to the hospital.

"It was rat poison and it disagreed with me," she said. "They gave it to me as a joke."

Chuck said he also had tried heroin. But he said he had found it harder to quit speed than "smack" (heroin).

"With smack," he said, "sooner or later you'll come to the attention of the authorities and get some help."

A young man with a seven-year history of using drugs said he had "blown his mind" dozens of times—that is, blown himself into a state of miserable immobility.

"I have attempted suicide three times in the last two years," he said. "They tell me speed will kill me, but they don't say when."

Yesterday he was in Dr. Dernburg's clinic consulting room, on the third painful day of trying once more to "come down" and rejoin the normal world.

What Do You Think?

Compare these accounts of drug use with the experiences reported in Readings 5, 6, 7, and 8. Based on these and other accounts with which you are familiar, how would you describe the "typical" drug user?

10. "IT'S SUCH AN EFFORT TO TALK" *

Reports on the effects of LSD have been conflicting. Both negative and positive reports exist in abundance. Here is the narrative of one person while under the influence of this drug:

It's such an effort to talk. I'm sorry it's such an effort to talk.

I'm seeing, as I said, pastel colors, green and pink and yellow, and

---

* Excerpted from John C. Pollard, Leonard Uhr, and Elizabeth Stern, *Drugs and Phantasy,* Boston, Mass.: Little, Brown & Company, 1965.

I feel like I'm being floated away, just floated away. Not like I was floating up and down on a rough shore like I felt before—there I am writhing again. Why must I writhe? I feel breathless, like I have to get my breath. Yet I feel very wide awake. If I could only breathe better! Ahhh. I would like to breathe better, I really would. My mouth feels like it's coming down, yet my voice is staying up there on a level plane. And it sounds so funny. Ohhh. I feel sort of wet now. Like I'm under water. I know my skin's not wet but I feel wet. I can't get my breath. Ohhh. I feel sort of like I'm just being pressed down upon so heavily, so very heavily. If I could only go to sleep. . . .

But it looks like I'm underwater, too, and I know I'm not underwater. This is very strange. My back hurts. The muscles are so tired and I keep moving around and hurting them, ever and ever, into infinitude, infinitude. If I could just go to sleep and get rid of all this static in my ears and this feeling that I have to close my eyes yet I have to keep them open at the same time yet there's nothing to see. It's most disturbing.

Maybe I'm on a dream, in a dream, I don't know. But I find it very hard to breathe. My tongue feels very odd to my teeth which also feel very big. . . . Looks like a lot of eyes looking at me, strange eyes like out of a comic book, dream. Oh, I wish I could get out from under this tremendous burden on my chest. Will it ever end, will it ever end?

What Do You Think?

How would you define this experience?

11. NINE, FIVE, TWO *

The next reading describes the responses of an individual, under the effects of LSD, when asked to perform certain memory tasks:

Repeat these digits forward: six, one, two.
    Six, one, two.
Six, one, five, eight.
    Six, one, five, eight.
Five, two, one, eight, six.
    Five, two, one, eight, six.
Now repeat these digits backwards: two, five, nine.
    Nine, five, two.

---

* Excerpted from John C. Pollard, Leonard Uhr, and Elizabeth Stern, *Drugs and Phantasy,* Boston, Mass.: Little, Brown & Company, 1965.

Eight, four, one, three.
    Three, four, one, eight.
Nine, seven, eight, five, two.
    Two, five, seven, one, nine. Still feels like something is pushing in my stomach. But not so hard now. Now I have a slight increase in the switching in the volume of the receiver . . .
In two minutes make as many words as you can from the word "Pleasure."
    Sure, please, sure, please . . .

What Do You Think?

1.   Would you accept this as evidence of the effects of LSD? Why or why not? Is it a "fair" test? Explain. Would you want to know any additional information about this subject? Explain.

2.   Would a person not under the influence of LSD be able to repeat the digits accurately? Try it yourself.

12. "THOSE SORES DON'T LOOK SO GOOD " *

Drug addiction can produce some sorry specimens. A reporter who accompanied two narcotic detectives on their rounds describes one such specimen:

Ray Viera is the larger, more volatile of the two detectives. His hair is wavy with streaks of gray, and he tends to tap your shoulder when he is involved in a statement. Burt Alvins is smaller, wiry; most of his head is a short gray-flecked crew cut.

We drive along 118th Street. The area crawls with big-city specialties: numbers, junk, whores. Garbage piles up in back, between the houses. The garbage men can't get in there because the backs are locked, so the stuff mounts and mounts, and every once in a while they make an assault and get some of it out, chasing away rats as big and careless as dogs.

"We have to go see somebody."

"One of our informers," Ray says. "This guy's not stupid. He's intelligent. He's a nice guy. Wait till you see him though."

---

* Excerpted from Bruce Jackson, "Exiles from the American Dream: The Junkie and the Cop," *The Atlantic Monthly*, January, 1967. © 1966, The Atlantic Monthly Company, Boston, Mass.

We enter a building just above Central Park. Someone lives on the first floor. The second, up the narrow dark stairway that is even darker after the bright sun, is vacant. All the doors are open; one is unhinged and lies flat in the room, as if something walked right in without bothering to stop. Another door hangs at a grotesque angle, the top hinge ripped off. More rubbish in there. A few empty bottles. We go up another flight, and Ray goes to Elmer's door. It is unlocked, and he eases it open slightly. Elmer is sitting on the bed, a blanket over his knees. "Anybody here?" Ray asks.

"No, I'm alone."

Ray waves us in. The room is about twelve by twelve. A big, old TV is on a bureau by the wall. A new Sony is on another bureau, turned on to a talk show. Elmer tells us a prostitute friend bought it for him as a present.

"How are your legs, Elmer?" Ray asks.

Elmer moves the blanket from his thighs. On both are long running sores, about four or five inches long and a half inch or so wide; they look deep; something oozes. . . .

Burt says, "Why don't you let us get you in the hospital for a while?"

"Maybe next week."

"Those sores don't look so good."

"I can't go in this week. You know."

"How are your arms?"

"Feel a little better." He holds his forearms out and moves the fingers. A Popeye caricature: from the elbows up, the arms are the thin sticks of an old man; below the elbow, they are swollen like thighs. The fingers all look like oversized thumbs. Like his thighs, Elmer's arms are covered with scars that look like strip photos of the surface of the moon. There are too many of the dime- and quarter-size craters to count.

"This is Bruce, Elmer. He's a new man, and we're breaking him in."

Elmer looks up, noticing or acknowledging me for the first time. He nods and shrugs. They make a date to meet somewhere later in the week.

"You sure you don't want us to get you in a hospital, Elmer?" Ray asks.

Elmer says no.

For me, Rays asks, "Elmer, what you shooting now?"

"About eight bags."

"When did you start?"

"1955."

"And how old are you now?"

"Forty-eight."

There's a silence, directed to me. Elmer looks sixty-five or seventy, and they all know I'd thought him an old man. He folds the blanket over his thighs, and we go out. On the way, Burt gives Elmer a few bucks and says get some cigarettes.

Going down the stairs, Ray says, "If he tells you he's shooting eight bags, that means he's shooting twelve. That's sixty bucks a day. Seven days a week. Four hundred and twenty dollars a week. Almost what I make a month." Elmer, obviously is in some business activities about which the police prefer not to ask.

Most New York addicts, I know, spend less than twenty dollars a day for narcotics. Few look as grim as Elmer. But enough do. And enough wind up dead because of infection or accidental overdose; many have TB. The physiological debilitation and destruction result from concomitants of drug taking: the junkie spends his money for drugs instead of food, his drugs are cut with quinine and other chemicals that often do him considerable damage, and worst of all, the material he injects and the instruments he uses are so unsanitary that he constantly risks the kinds of infection that have scarred Elmer. The junk itself, so long as it does not exceed the addict's tolerance, is not really as physiologically harmful as cigarettes or alcohol, but the life style is vicious.

"Some of these guys," Burt says, "they get worse than Elmer. Ruin all the veins in the arms and legs, burn them out, and they shoot in the mouth. And when that goes, in the penis. Hurts like hell, they say, but they can find the vein."

I ask them if their visiting Elmer's apartment in daylight might not get him into trouble with other addicts. They say no, they spend a lot of time questioning addicts, most of whom are not informers, standard procedure.

"These people around here—they know who you are?"

"Sure, they know us. Even if they'd never seen us before, they'd know us. If you're white around here, you're either a bill collector or the Man. They maybe don't know which Man you are, but you're one of them."

What Do You Think?

1. Why do you suppose Elmer wouldn't go to the hospital?
2. What factors might lead a person like Elmer to such a condition?
3. How would you suggest that we help people like Elmer?

13. AN EARLY REPORT ON THE EFFECTS OF MARIHUANA *

In 1938 Mayor La Guardia of the City of New York asked the New York Academy of Medicine to investigate the effects of the drug marihuana. The Academy's report, often referred to as the La Guardia report, has not been widely disseminated. Listed below are eight conclusions from the report. Many have been contradicted by more recent research. How would you account for such differences in opinion?

1. Smoking marihuana does not lead directly to mental or physical deterioration.
2. The habitual smoker knows when to stop, as excessive doses reverse the drug's usually pleasant effects.
3. Marihuana does not lead to addiction (in the medical sense) and while it is naturally habit-forming, its withdrawal does not lead to the horrible withdrawal symptoms of the opiates.
4. No deaths have ever been recorded that can be ascribed to marihuana.
5. Marihuana is not a direct causal factor in sexual or criminal misconduct.
6. Juvenile delinquency is not caused by marihuana smoking, although the two are sometimes associated.
7. The publicity concerning the catastrophic effects of marihuana smoking in New York is unfounded.
8. It is more of a nuisance than a menace.

What Do You Think?

1. What kind of reactions do you think this report might receive today?
2. Why do you suppose that the report has not been widely circulated?
3. How might you determine the validity of this report?

14. MORE EFFECTS OF DRUG USE

What are the effects of drugs? Reactions vary. Evidence appears contradictory. Here are a variety of examples:

---

* Excerpted from Norman Taylor, *Narcotics, Nature's Dangerous Gifts,* New York, N. Y.: Dell Publishing Co., 1966.

[A 29-year-old addict who switched from heroin to Methedrine:]

George is clean-shaven, dapper with tight-white jeans, 29 years old, cocksure with a lot to learn. "I was tripping with smack (using heroin off and on) in the service at 19. Got busted for it good at twenty-two," says George with the attitude of the con-wise addict. "I had three years of Nalline (a narcotics test often used for addicts on probation), so I started using 'garbage can' drugs, a little of anything I could get. I'm one dope addict who always knew how to hold down a real job; a bartender, high class places too, and I always worked, even while I was on junk. Good jobs, good pay, plenty to buy all the speed I wanted.

So, I made probation shooting crystal all the time. I'd shoot a lot of speed, get real wired up then shoot a lot of yellow jackets. I'd run on speed, stop along the run with four or five yellow jackets and do it all over again. Anytime I'd drive I had one drink. A cop stopped me; who wants to hassle with a bartender with a little booze on his breath.

My last job was big with twenty-two people in this bar working for me; and a few months ago I got hung-up with my old lady so I quit and spent full time just shooting dope. I went on the run for 18 days. No sleep, no food, nothing, just shooting meth, high every minute. Finally I busted my old lady's jaw and got picked up. They put me in a padded cell, treated me like I was righteously crazy and man I was, a nut in a nut house.

I came up here and saw people who were even worse off than me, so now I'm beginning to think, maybe I'm not so goddamn smart as I figured and I'm weak. A lot too weak. So weak I'll probably be the last methhead out of here.[1]

[Dr. Donald Louria, a physician in New York City:]

Used promiscuously and under uncontrolled circumstances, LSD is extremely dangerous. It is absolutely unpredictable. Of the 114 cases hospitalized at the Bellevue Hospital during a recent 18 month period, 13 per cent entered the hospital with overwhelming panic. There was uncontrolled violence in 12 per cent and nearly 9 per cent had attempted either homicide or suicide. Of the whole 114, almost 14 per cent had to be sent on to long term mental hospitalization, and, surprisingly enough, half of those had no previous history of underlying psychiatric disorder. . . .

Further, LSD has another danger not adequately emphasized. A small but growing number of people who take LSD repeatedly withdraw

---

[1] Excerpted from David Perlman, "The Games that "Meth" Heads Play," *San Francisco Chronicle*, December 7, 1967.

from society. They engage in perpetual introspective orgies, lead a totally drug oriented life, become negativistic and unconstructive. These people are beginning to worry even some of the proponents of LSD. If the group becomes much larger, it could conceivably be a substantial danger to society as a whole. . . .

There is not one whit of evidence that heroin users are given to man-to-man violence. Their crimes are more against property. In New York City, some 20 per cent to 30 per cent of such crimes are committed by heroin addicts; it has been estimated that they steal up to one billion dollars worth of goods a year to support their habit." [2]

[The following is from a United Press newspaper story from Washington, D. C.:]

A doctor told Congress today that there is evidence that the drug LSD can significantly increase the chance of cancer. The witness, Dr. Cecil B. Jacobson of George Washington University Medical School, told the house hearing that the hallucinogenic drug also can cause deformed babies, mutations of future generations and premature aging of cells. Emphasizing his findings were primary and based on a small group, Jacobson said nonetheless "the evidence is now rather substantial that chromosomal breakage occurs" among women who took LSD and in their offspring.

Dr. Jacobson said evidence was building that LSD or any other agent that causes chromosomes to break, . . . will shorten cell life in the user and "significantly increase the chance of cancer." Jacobson said that there was reason to anticipate a high incidence of leukemia among LSD users of future years. Jacobson said there was also evidence that LSD taken during pregnancy may cause abnormal babies. In addition, he said the drug could cause genetic changes that may not show up for several years or even generations.[3]

[A psychologist's views on marihuana:]

Cannabis is an hallucinogen whose effects are somewhat similar to, though much milder than, peyote and LSD. The confirmed user takes it daily or more frequently, and through experience and careful regulation of the dose is able to consistently limit the effects to euphoria and other desired qualities. Unlike peyote, there are typically no claims of benefit other than the immediate effects. Mild tolerance and physical dependence may develop when the more potent preparations are used to excess;

[2] Excerpted from D. B. Louria, "Cool Talk About Drugs," *The New York Times Magazine,* August 6, 1967. © 1967 by The New York Times Company. Reprinted by permission.

[3] "LSD Link to Cancer, Deformed Babies Made," Marin (County) *Independent Journal* (California), February 19, 1968.

however, they are virtually nonexistent for occasional or moderate regular users. There are apparently no deleterious physical effects resulting from moderate use, though excessive indulgence noted in some Eastern countries contributes to a variety of ailments. The most serious hazard is the precipitation of transient psychoses. Unstable individuals may experience a psychotic episode from even a small amount, and although they typically recover within a few days, some psychoses triggered by cannabis reactions may last for several months. In Eastern countries, where cannabis is taken in large amounts, some authors feel that it is directly responsible for a sizable portion of the intakes in psychiatric hospitals.

In this country cannabis is not used to excess by Eastern standards; however, it does attract a disproportionate number of poorly adjusted and non-productive young persons in the lower socio-economic strata. . . . In Eastern countries cannabis use is currently also more prevalent in the lower classes; however, moderate use is not illegal, socially condemned, or necessarily considered indicative of personality defects. The reputation of cannabis for inciting major crimes is unwarranted and it probably has no more effect than alcohol in this respect. . . .

Laws controlling marihuana are similar or identical to those pertaining to the opiates, including the mandatory imposition of long prison sentences for certain offenses. Many judges have complained that these laws have resulted in excessive sentences (five to ten years) for relatively minor offenses with marihuana. The 1962 White House Conference made the following recommendation:

"It is the opinion of the Panel that the hazard of marihuana per se have been exaggerated and that long criminal sentences imposed on an occasional user or possessor are in poor social perspective." [4]

[The position of the American Medical Association and the National Research Council on marihuana:]

The notion that marihuana is safer for the user than alcohol, or at least no worse, has become one of the soothing and glibly repeated clichés of the day. Increasing numbers of medical men agree with it, among them James L. Goddard, who recently resigned as commissioner of the Food and Drug Administration. Alarmed by widespread and often unverified acceptance of the idea, the A. M. A. and the National Research Council last week took a joint pot-shot at the drug in what the A. M. A. called a "major position paper" (translation: a report that falls just short of being official A. M. A. policy).

Medical research into the effects of marihuana is still in its infancy—

---

[4] Excerpted from W. H. McGlothlin, "Cannabis: A Reference," *The Marihuana Papers,* David Solomon, ed., Indianapolis, Indiana: The Bobbs-Merrill Company, Inc., 1966.

so much so that last week's condemnation had to be based on the same sparse evidence that others have used to support the use, and legalization, of the drug. The major difference, therefore, was one of perspective and emphasis.

It is well established that the use of marihuana does not produce physical dependence, but can result in psychological dependence. Advocates of legalized marihuana concede this, but add that already disturbed users are more likely than others to develop such dependence. The A.M.A.-N.R.C. report makes no such distinctions; by merely pointing out that the drug can cause psychological dependence, it implied that it should be avoided.

Those who use marihuana to excess, it is known, run the risk of lessened intellectual activity. Pot partisans point out that those who use alcohol to excess not only lessen intellectual activity but cause damage to the brain, liver and heart as well. The A.M.A.-N.R.C. report contents itself with pointing out that social productivity is reduced in those areas of Asia, Africa, and South America where heavy use of marihuana is common.

The purified and concentrated active ingredient of marihuana, tetrahydrocannabinol (THC), can cause the same sort of hallucinogenic symptoms as LSD. Pro-marihuana physicians point out that THC is in such limited experimental production and is so difficult to synthesize, that few if any marihuana users are likely to get their hands on it. The A.M.A. feels that any LSD-like drug, in any concentration, should not be available to the public.

Hashish, a form of marihuana with an extremely high concentration of the hemp plant resin that gives a stick its kick, is more dangerous than the garden variety of "grass" generally available in the U. S. Pro-marihuana advocates admit this, but argue that legally available marihuana would lessen the appeal of hashish. The A.M.A.-N.R.C. report predicts that any relaxation of anti-marihuana laws would encourage an even heavier illegal traffic in hashish, than that at present.

While condemning the use of marihuana and supporting strict penalties for those who sell it, the statement calls present penalties for possession of pot "unrealistic." First offenders, who now face up to ten years in prison for possession, should not be treated harshly, the medical groups recommend. Only penalties for second and third offenses, they add, should be made gradually more severe. And they feel that "additional research is needed to determine more about the effects of marihuana" before anyone should make up his mind about it.[5]

---

[5] "Marijuana Warning," *Time* Magazine, June 28, 1968. Copyright Time, Inc. 1968.

[The director of the National Institute of Mental Health:]

"Alienation," which he called a major underlying cause of drug abuse, "is deeper and more diffuse now than in any previous period of American history."

Dr. Stanley F. Yolles said the problem—which he defined as "rebellion without a cause, rejection without a program and a refusal of what is without a vision of what should be"—deserves urgent attention.

"If this is not done, there are serious dangers that large proportions of current and future generations will reach adulthood embittered toward the larger society, unequipped to take on parental, vocational and other citizen roles, and involved in some form of socially deviant behavior.[6]

Born With a Craving For Drugs *

He is a beautiful baby, dimpled and darling, with a fuzz of dark hair topping his well-shaped head.

But within hours of his birth he's screaming and twitching and the anxious nurse has called the pediatrician back to his side.

"Yes," agreed the nurse after the doctor had checked the baby and the mother's records as well, "yes, she does need a lot of pain killers . . . and they don't seem to help her at all."

Seconds later the doctor is in the new mother's room.

"What are you hooked on?" he screams.

"Do I have to tell you the truth?" she asks.

"Yes. If you want your baby to live."

He is a beautiful baby, dimpled and darling, but now he's fighting for his life. He's experiencing withdrawal symptoms that are possibly every bit as racking as those that would torture his mother or any other drug abuser if they were suddenly deprived of the drug they crave.

He's suffering from neonatal addiction—an inheritance passed on by his mother the same way the vitamins she might take pass through the placenta barrier.

His is a confirmed case; his mother admitted it.

But there are many, many more cases pediatricians can't confirm. There are enough so that at Jackson Hospital here "any baby who presents unusual behavior at birth, at least at this institution, is suspect," says Dr. Doralys Arias, instructor in the department of pediatrics, who also saw 10 confirmed cases there last year—cases so overt it was known in advance the mother was an addict.

---

[6] Excerpted from the *San Francisco Chronicle,* March 7, 1968.
* Janet Chusmir, "Born with a Craving for Drugs," Associated Press, *San Francisco Sunday Examiner and Chronicle,* November 10, 1968.

They're getting to be a more common sight in the nursery—these babies born with a craving for drugs. They're increasing with the availability of different kinds of drugs and the abuse of them. "Defined broadly," one doctor points out, "a lot of people are taking a lot of things and a lot of them affect their babies."

How it affects them is a variable. Some just don't look well. Some have bad color. Some fail to thrive. Others are irritable, or twitch, or jerk. Or go into convulsions. Or stop breathing.

Their symptoms will vary depending on the drug the mother is taking—whether it's heroin or morphine she's addicted to, or amphetamines, barbituates, psychotherapeutic drugs or a myriad of combinations she's misusing. It will depend, along with the drugs, on dosage, frequency of use and the maturity of the infant at birth.

Untreated, they'll die, says Dr. Louis Gluck, professor of pediatrics at the University of Miami's School of Medicine. "Treated, most will live, but some will die."

The treatment is other drugs, generally thorazine, one of the tranquilizers used for psychotherapy. It's given to the infant orally, or intravenously if he can't take it by mouth, to relieve the symptoms of withdrawal.

"Sometimes it can take up to six months to withdraw a baby," says Dr. Arias. "The average is three months."

Compounding the problem at times is the difficulty of detecting it in advance. There's hope that someday, in the near future, some procedure will be designed to pick out the expectant mother who is abusing drugs. Even today, certain psychotherapeutic drugs can be detected through chemical urine analysis.

Usually the mother who is using a needle to feed her addiction has the marks to give doctors the clue. "But not always," says Dr. Arias, "they're also remarkably clever about hiding the sites."

Some women don't realize that excesses in various drugs are as serious to the baby they carry within them as heroin or morphine. "But it's excesses we're speaking of," the doctors point out. "We don't want to panic the woman who is taking drugs under a doctor's care."

It is not these women, but the increasing numbers of others addicted to hard narcotics or habituated to other drugs, who are the increasing concern of those who deal with them and their babies.

Miss Rachel Erwin, director of Social Services for the Dade Public Health Department's Maternal and Infant Care Project, is one such concerned person, because "We used to hear of one or two a year, now we're seeing about one a week—women who are admitting to drugs of all kinds."

Mothers who are mainliners often bring other "gifts" to their unborn babies along with neonatal addiction she says. "Since they know little about sterile procedures, we see hepatitis and other diseases which have disastrous effects on pregnancies."

What Do You Think?

> As you can see, reports on drug effects differ considerably. With this in mind, how would you answer an individual who asked you whether or not he should use drugs? Explain.

15. THE MAJOR DRUGS USED *

The following reading is a summary of each of the major drugs or drug groups and their effects.

1. *Narcotic analgetic drugs:* "Narcotic" is a general term which is defined as a condition of stupor or insensibility and which, in the field of medicine, has come to mean those compounds (e.g. heroin, morphine) capable of producing analgesia (pain relief) and of causing psychological and physical dependence. A number of these drugs can be extracted from the poppy seed (the crude extract is called opium) including morphine and codeine. . . .

In addition to the drugs that can be extracted from the opium plant, chemists have been able to synthesize a large number of compounds which possess all the properties of the opium derivatives. Such drugs as Demerol ®, Percodan ®, and Prinadol ® have been produced synthetically and, as far as can be determined, have similar effects. . . . The effects on the central nervous system are of prime importance. A person becomes drowsy, unresponsive to his environment, and mentally "foggy" under the influence of these narcotic drugs. Remember that the use of the term narcotics here is applied specifically to that group represented by heroin, morphine, and Demerol ® and is not meant to include all drugs that depress or affect a person's mind. The mental effects that are produced lead to apathy, lethargy, and even unconcern for such basic necessities as food and cleanliness. The whole spectrum of drug action may best be called a state of euphoria—an abnormal or exaggerated sense of well-being (psychiatric definition). . . .

Most users of the narcotic drugs inject a solution of the drug directly

---

* Walter L. Way, M. D.

into the vein (intravenously), for greater and faster results, but many users will take the drug by injection into other sites, or will take pills by mouth. . . .

2. *The barbiturates and related hypnotic-sedative drugs:* The barbiturates have been available for over 60 years and represent a large, well-studied group of drugs. In addition, a multitude of compounds have been produced which possess similar action and which should be classed along with the barbiturates. In the strict medical sense, these drugs (depending on the dosage) cause a depression of the brain which can vary from a mild sedative (calming) action to coma. As sedatives, they are often prescribed by doctors. The danger lies in continuing usage after the medical reason has passed, or in increasing the dose (if one pill helped that much, why not take two?). . . .

The barbiturates are sometimes combined with other potentially addicting drugs, particularly Dexedrine ®. The combination of barbiturates with sympathomimetic amines like Methedrine and amphetamine is probably favored by the abuser because it tends to reduce the jitteriness and uneasiness produced by the sympathomimetic amines alone. . . .

3. *Sympathomimetic amines:* Included in this class are a number of compounds best represented by Benzedrine ® (amphetamine), Dexedrine ® (dextroamphetamine), and Methedrine ® (methamphetamine). These drugs are frequently prescribed for an individual with weight problems since they decrease the appetite. They are also used for individuals in various states of mental depression. Others have begun using the amphetamines for the sole purpose of achieving the increasing mental alertness and sense of euphoria which they produce. . . .

In sensitive persons, psychotic symptoms may result, sometimes after a single large dose (50–75 mg) of the drug. This mental state frequently resembles a typical schizophrenic [1] reaction and includes visual and auditory hallucinations and paranoic [2] tendencies, though the individual still remains oriented as to time and place. The withdrawal of the amphetamines does not result in changes which could be called a withdrawal syndrome since they are very mild compared to those symptoms observed following use of the barbiturates. These drugs are used in a number of different forms but primarily by "mainlining" (intravenous injection) or by taking tablets orally (Dexedrine).

4. *Cocaine:* This is a compound which produces a variety of changes in the human body. Its abuse centers about its ability to cause

---

[1] Schizophrenia is a psychosis.
[2] Paranoia is a mental disorder characterized by delusions of persecution and one's own greatness.

mental changes similar to those seen with the amphetamines. The mental stimulation produced is a marked euphoria and feeling of great mental and physical capability. The same toxicity can be achieved with this drug as with the amphetamines. The incidence of abuse in the United States is very low.

5. *Marihuana; Marijuana:* The source of the drug is the flowering top of the female hemp plant. Recent research indicates that the compound 1–$\triangle$ tetrahydrocannabinol is one of the active ingredients which produce the hallucinogenic action of the plant.

It is interesting that the personality . . . of the user has a great deal to do with the effects obtained. Most consistently marihuana produces a drowsy state of mind. . . . There may be a distortion of time, place, and memory. Very familiar knowledge may become unfamiliar, whereas the unfamiliar seems to become very familiar. Hallucinatory effects may be varied and include synesthesia (where a given sensation is perceived as a sensation of a different sense, as when a sound produces a sensation of color), and audio and visual aberrations.

Mood alterations are frequent and the individual may experience feelings of well being, great joy, and exultation, which are frequently called "the high" by regular users. Increasing doses may give a sense of panic and impending doom, and some observers feel that a toxic psychosis may result when the personality of the person taking marihuana is predisposed to such psychotic events. This means that a basic and underlying mental problem may be revealed in the presence of a large enough dose of this drug. The same effects may be seen with other psychotomimetic drugs such as LSD, mescaline, and psilocybin. . . .

The plant is usually cut, dried and finely chopped to make cigarettes which, when smoked, produce effects within a few minutes. These effects last some twenty to thirty minutes. . . .

6. *Lysergic acid derivatives:* Most familiar of this group is LSD (lysergic acid diethylamide) which is one of the strongest drugs known to man. A dose of 100 to 200 *micrograms* will produce very significant psychic effects in an average person. . . .

LSD 25 is produced by chemical synthesis of the diethylamide portion and the lysergic acid portion. Lysergic acid is a natural product of an ergot fungus (Claviceps purpurea) which grows on rye and other grains. . . . The synthesis of LSD from scratch is a complicated task, but, since lysergic acid is readily available, transformation into LSD is much simpler to accomplish. . . .

The action of this drug (and for that matter all psychotomimetics) which most interests us is that affecting one's actions, which are best described as alterations in mood, perception, and behavior. . . .

Death can result from LSD use since the drug can cause respiratory failure. In addition, LSD can produce severe reactions in borderline psychotic and depressed patients. At least three types of reactions have been noted including: 1) acute reactions, 2) recurrent reactions, and 3) prolonged effects. The individual may tend towards acute paranoia and confusion, which may lead to dangerous behavior and suicide. It is also possible that a panic state may develop as a possible reaction to the ingestion of the drug and the effects that it produces. Recurrent reactions are analogous to the acute reaction but may occur up to a year after taking the drug. The chronic reactions are most disturbing because of the persistent anxiety that the individual experiences, which may be enhanced by visual aberrations. . . . The duration of this chronic state is variable from weeks to months, and treatment with drugs or psychotherapy is frequently unsuccessful. The alterations in mental processes and perceptive ability coupled with a significantly diminished ability to control emotions . . . are the real hazards of these compounds.

Mental withdrawal or clearcut dependence syndrome cannot be shown with LSD or for that matter with any of the other hallucinogenic drugs that we will talk about.

Most scientists are agreed that the potential for genetic damage or chromosomal alteration is present with LSD, but, unfortunately, so is such potential present with most drugs. The description of alterations occurring in cultures of cells showing chromosomal changes probably is factual. Whether this situation actually exists in life is still a debatable point and one which to date has not been answered. . . . Further research in this area is a vital necessity.

7. *Mescaline:* From the Mexican cactus comes the active hallucinogen mescaline. Indians in the Southwestern United States and Northeastern Mexico have long used this plant (called peyotyl by the Aztecs) as a means of producing alterations in mood . . . in various tribal religious ceremonies. The Apache Indians of this area used the buttons (pods) of peyote for the same purpose (see Reading 6). The user experiences visual illusions and hallucinations closely resembling those of LSD. Toxic reactions, of acute anxiety and panic, appear to be dependent on dose and the personality of the user. As with LSD, there seems to be little chance of true addiction or physical dependence. The drug is usually ingested by chewing the pods.

8. *STP:* This compound is a synthetic chemical related to the amphetamine family (Methedrine, Dexedrine) that produces psychic effects similar to mescaline but is some 40 to 50 times more powerful than mescaline. Originally synthetized by the Dow Chemical Company and called "DOM," it was looked upon as a possible superior hallucinogen with a more intense action and a longer duration. . . . As expected, many intense reactions occurred and use of the compound dropped because

of these toxic reactions. The letters STP are said to stand for serenity, tranquility, and peace. Others have said that STP stands for the familiar oil product and represents a compound that will "make your motor run better."

9. *MDA:* MDA is similar in chemical structure to STP and is capable of LSD-like effects. This drug seems to give a euphoria rather than the depression seen when a person is "coming down" from LSD. The oral dosage needed to produce these effects is quite large and one death has been associated with the use of MDA in combination with other drugs.

10. *Psilocybin:* The mushroom (Psilocybe Mexicana Heim) is a source of psilocybin, a hallucinogen capable of giving effects very similar to LSD. This orally active compound is very similar to another hallucinogen derived from the skin of toads called "Bufotenin," which is not active orally. A third similar compound is N'N-dimethyltryptamine (DMT). Since DMT lacks oral effectiveness, it is used intravenously and will produce a fairly intense but brief effect, which is frequently called the "businessmen's trip."

11. *Sernyl ® (PCP) (peace pill):* This is a drug that has been tested in clinical medicine as a sedative and general anesthetic. It was rejected because of its tendency to cause hallucinations, delusions, and, possibly, a depressed state.

12. *Ololiuqui:* This substance is derived from a plant species related to the morning glory and is known to contain D-lysergic acid monoethylamide, a close chemical relative to LSD. This substance has been, for generations, part of the religious practice of a number of tribes of American and Mexican Indians.

13. *Nutmeg:* This household spice, when taken orally and in a dose equivalent to two grated nutmegs, produces mental changes resembling those of marihuana. The long period between taking the drug and getting its effects, along with severe liver damage that may result, tend to limit use of this drug.

ACTIVITIES FOR INVOLVEMENT

1.   The difficulty in measuring the magnitude of any problem is frequently the lack of a precise "measuring stick." Consider methods by which the drug problem could be evaluated as to size, type of drug used, age of user, family and personal background, etc. How could you measure the extent of drug use among your friends and in your school? What aspects of drug use might make collection of such data difficult? Discuss.

2.   What elements of the statistics given in this chapter are most subject to error? Develop your own set of statistics by polling your local community. Try to collect data such as: what drugs are used, how long they have been used, has the user moved from less potent drugs to more

potent ones, and what is the source of the drugs? What difficulties would you expect to encounter in attempting to gather such data?

3.   Invite a number of experts on drug usage (a minister, a youth worker, a doctor, a narcotics officer) to discuss with the class what characteristics of a drug besides those such as cost and availability might determine who uses it or to what extent it is used.

4.   Hold a class discussion on the question: "How can fruitful discussion on drugs in our community be provoked?" How can the kind of atmosphere be produced that will generate mutual trust and respect so that talk can flow?

5.   It has been observed that girls are more likely to be guilty of a "nark" (narcotics police) charge than of other delinquency charges such as burglary, assault, or civil disturbances. It has been argued that girls are more capable of taking drugs than they are of committing other delinquent acts. Would you agree? Why or why not?

6.   Part of your learning about drugs and their use should include hearing from and knowing the people who use drugs. Ask a representative from Synanon, Alcoholics Anonymous, or another self-help group to describe their techniques to the class. Consider the methods that they utilize to get at a person's problem. Might their methods be useful for dealing with other kinds of problems as well?

7.   Review the readings in this chapter and then draw up a list of reasons for drug use. Then do some further reading. Rather than deciding that one person suffered "family problems" or "boredom," try to discover as best you can what the specific circumstances of an individual's problems were. If the article you are considering does not provide sufficient information, consult a number of additional sources in the library. Compare your list with those compiled by other class members. What similarities and differences do you notice?

Next, take each suggested cause and suggest a possible means of solution. Save these for rethinking and possible reformulation after you have read Chapter 6.

8.   The question above assumes—wrongly, perhaps—that in each case under consideration there was a problem which led the person, almost directly, to drug use as a solution of that problem. What of those people who turn to drugs not for relief, but rather for pleasure? Assuming that high school students have about the same exposure to drugs, what reasons can you suggest for the fact that some use drugs while others do not?

9.   What part does the presence or absence of physical dependence play in drug use? It has been argued by many that most drugs are used for their psychic effects. The fact that they profoundly influence the body in other ways, however, cannot be ignored. From the readings presented as well as others listed in the bibliography, draw up a set of criteria by which to evaluate the potential physical danger that might result from the use of these drugs. Consider not only the drug action itself but the paraphernalia used to take the drug, the influence of the drug on normal functioning of the body, and the influences exerted on the ability of the user to carry out normal day-to-day tasks.

Why Do
People Use Drugs?

4

In the activities following the last chapter you were asked to think of some reasons why people use drugs. There certainly is no one cause but rather a variety of contributing factors. This chapter presents several accounts to illustrate why and how some people made the decision to use drugs.

1. FORCED INTO THOSE CIRCUMSTANCES *

A newcomer to the drug scene expresses how he came to be involved and his feelings about such involvement.

You come to San Francisco and don't know anyone. You need a place to sleep, so do other people. You get together; someone has an apartment—several people sleep there. If you stay awhile you scuffle around and hustle up some money to help with the rent and food. You have acquired friends; they too have been forced into these circumstances. You have a common bond of destitution. Hustling and scuffling brings you into illegitimate activities such as prostitution, theft and the use and sale of drugs. Drugs are illegal, and they make you feel good. Sharing a "joint" is not only illegal, it is familiar; sharing an outfit is even more illegal and more familiar. You have an even stronger bond of association with more friends. You are a "dope fiend" and only you and your new friends know what's happening really. The people in the home town would never understand and they wouldn't be able to make it in the

---

* Excerpted from *Drugs in the Tenderloin,* Central City Multi-Service Center, 272 Sixth Street, San Francisco, California, 1967.

"Big City" where things are really happening. Three months ago you didn't know what dope was and now you have your own little outfit bag, you can recognize a cop a block away, you know a new language, you've read some books on drugs and you've done a thousand and one forbidden things. You are a righteous doper! Someone asks you if you want to eat and you say I just want to get high. You become "strung out" on a way of life and I mean strung out. You can't talk to anyone else outside of your sub-culture "they wouldn't understand." You had square friends three months ago that you could tell anything to and now you wouldn't know what to say to them. Your front door is locked as securely as any cell door. You are playing a role and you think you are important enough for the police to be watching your place. Even if you don't think that the Narks [police] are watching, it makes the game more exciting to act as if they were. It is fashionable to say you're paranoid. You know "what's happening," but you don't know what month it is or whether it is day or night.

What Do You Think?

1. Would you agree that anyone outside of the drug subculture "wouldn't understand"? Why or why not?

2. What does the author mean when he says "only you and your friends know what's happening really"?

2. MIDDLE-CLASS KIDS AND DRUGS *

A group of high school students in a suburb north of San Francisco expresses various viewpoints on drug use in a typical "middle-class society."

I've been coming here every day, trying to figure out why I use drugs. I know all the bad things they do to you. I listen, then I go home at night and get stoned. Why?

The blond-haired speaker, about to enter his senior year of high school, was one of 11 teen-agers who gathered . . . last week for one of the closing sessions of an extraordinary summer school class.

For the students, freshmen through seniors, and their teacher, it was a day for contemplating the success or failure of the pilot course.

The class, which never met in a school room, was called DIG, an

---

* Excerpted from Stephen Cook, "Experimental Summer Course Investigates Teen Drug Use," Marin County (California) *Independent Journal,* July 22, 1968.

acronym for Drug Investigatory Group. Educators thought it could be the forerunner to an all-out classroom attack on what many adults consider to be the biggest teen-age problem—growing drug abuse.

DIG members asked that their real names not appear . . . , so the blond-haired speaker will be called Kenneth. In slowly spoken, precisely chosen words, he seemed to question the value of the course, saying he still does not know why he uses drugs.

Obviously disturbed by having recently learned that LSD may damage his chromosomes, Kenneth worried that he still hasn't stopped using acid.

"I've probably ruined all my children by now," he said. "I've taken 42 trips."

But the youth's attitude toward drugs was ambivalent. While remorseful about not stopping, he was also anxious to share with the group the fine experiences he has had with LSD and marihuana.

"I remember my first acid trip. It was at school in December 1965. My friend was just smiling so much and I asked him. 'Are you blowing weed?' and he showed me this powder and said 'No, it's this, LSD.' and I said I wanted some.

"He gave me some of the powder and I had heard nothing bad about LSD so I just went into the bathroom and swallowed it and it was really great, a beautiful trip."

Carrie's attitude toward drugs was also a little mixed up. At one moment, she talked of the beauty of blowing grass. A minute later she announced that she was "not going to turn on anymore." It's a deceit.

"I decided yesterday. I was stoned and sitting on the steps in Sausalito and, all of a sudden, I didn't want to be stoned anymore. The whole day was a bummer."

Charles, who talked of his own experiences with drugs and acid, said any drug abuse education course should also cover the evils of other drugs, particularly alcohol.

And just as alcohol is not separable from the drug education curriculum, neither is communication, said the students.

"There are so many walls. People don't talk anymore. They just build walls. They build walls to avoid talking about drugs, about Viet Nam. Parents and their children build walls so they can't talk to each other," Kenneth said.

Kenneth said he started breaking down the barriers with his parents when he came home one night and announced that "I'm stoned on LSD, Dad."

"Father flipped," he said, "But I've done it so many times now that we're starting to talk. While I'm on a trip, I'll say things that he understands and appreciates."

Christine said she might be able to do that with her father, but never with her mother.

"Mother never understands. She just says I'm wrong and we end up in an argument, yelling at each other. We can't even have small talk," she said.

Carrie said it sounded like Christine was building walls too, but Christine insisted that she wants to talk to her mother.

"Did it ever occur to you that your mother wants just as desperately to talk with you as you do with her?" asked Carrie.

During the discussion, the teen-agers became most excited when Carrie complained that Marin County is a very hard place to quit using drugs.

"It's everywhere. You can't avoid it, that wonderful sweet smell of grass," Carrie said.

"Yes, I've been walking down the sidewalk and smelled it. I walked back through some bushes, past some trees and found it, too, in a group, being passed around," said Kenneth, excited, talking much faster.

Soon the students were recounting their good trips and teacher Cyril Beattie stopped the discussion and said, "This disturbs me. You're all turning each other on with this talk. It sounds like a put-on."

And Kenneth, more slowly, less excited now, agreed: "Yes. We were tripping out. I've noticed this thing in myself when I think of drugs. It's the jet set, the in-crowd image. I wonder why that is?"

What Do You Think?

1. How would you answer Kenneth's question (in the last paragraph in this reading)?

2. Kenneth states "There are so many walls." What does he mean? Might this have something to do with drug use? Explain.

3. ARE DRUGS AN ESCAPE? *

A young high school student says that drugs are an escape. But an escape from what?

This thing about the rebellious teen-ager is just too much. Another reason for taking drugs is an escape. These are trying times for a teen-ager, pressure from society, parents and friends. Drugs are more easily available, they are a new experience, a new kick just like alcohol. You can say the

---

* Excerpted from the *Narcotics Inquiry Report,* San Mateo County (California) Juvenile Justice Commission, November, 1967.

same about adults who have a few drinks in the evening just to escape. Those who use drugs to a greater extent and for the fun of trying some new kick are emotionally ill. Drugs are a problem when you look at people like Leary. The problem is based on lack of education of adults as well as youth. The general public should be well informed. Legalize marihuana for adults like alcohol. The only problem is from the medical standpoint. Life is so very routine that some type of kick is actually needed. It's not wrong to look for a kick; less sensationalism, more true medical facts. Adults are permitted to drink alcohol and drive on the freeway and get killed. Marihuana will become popular. Why are alcohol and tobacco legal and not marihuana? What is morality? You are too young to go to work and maintain your own apartment, but you are expected to assume the responsibility of going to war and killing others. Who determines when an individual is of age? Why twenty-one?

What Do You Think?

1. Would you agree with the author that with life so routine, some type of kick is actually needed? If you do not agree, how would you respond to his statement?

2. Are these times more "trying" than earlier times? Why or why not?

3. The author states that drugs are an escape. Would you agree? Explain.

4. HOW DO I KNOW THAT DRUGS ARE BAD UNTIL I TRY THEM? *

Here is yet another viewpoint. Does this suggest a reason why some people use drugs?

You rationalize this way, when I was young they told me sex was bad. I tried it, it was good; so, how do I know that drugs are bad until I try them? The more you are told that a certain thing is bad, the more likely it is that you will try it out to find out for yourself. If you like the kicks, the trip, you do it again and again.

---

* Excerpted from *Drugs in the Tenderloin,* Central City Multi-Service Center, 272 Sixth Street, San Francisco, California, 1967.

What Do You Think?

1. How would you answer the question asked in the title to this reading?

2. A high school senior in California remarked that "It is harder and harder to resist trying marihuana." What would you say to her?

5. "MY BROTHER . . . INTRODUCED ME TO A COUPLE OF HIS FRIENDS " *

A 19-year-old relates how he started with marihuana and went on to morphine, cocaine, and Methedrine:

Because my father was in the navy, our family travelled all over Europe till I was nearly fifteen years old. After my father retired, we returned to the United States and moved to Southern California. It was here I got into my first serious trouble with the police. I had stolen a car and there was a warrant out for my arrest. Besides this, the town we were living in was a drag. After 8:00 at night it was like a morgue. So my older brother and I ran away to San Francisco. My brother had been in San Francisco before, so he introduced me to a couple of his friends who were pill pushers. He got hold of some weed and pretty soon I was fairly well hung-up on both pills and weed. Weed and pills got to be a bore after a while and a friend of mine turned me on to some morphine. Within six months I had a $50–$60 per day habit. I was making just enough money to pay for the habit and little else. My brother finally got me to kick the habit cold turkey. I was clean for nearly two and one-half months then got turned on to some "coke" and "smack." I dug them more than anything else I already had. Since I was pushing again, I figured I could get away with murder. Another six to seven months and I had about a $75 per day habit between the two of them. This time, because my health was so messed up from the last time, I committed myself to a private hospital so I could withdraw normally, rather than cold turkey. A month later I was released. I was too young to get a job and actually didn't want one. I was making a hell of a lot of money pushing weed, smack and coke. In fact, at one time I was making $400–$500 a week profit.

* Excerpted from *Drugs in the Tenderloin,* Central City Multi-Service Center, 272 Sixth Street, San Francisco, California, 1967.

What Do You Think?

What factors caused this individual to use drugs?

6.   "I'VE GOT A MONKEY ON MY BACK" *

An ex-football player describes what drug use did for him.

I'm a drug addict, but actually I began as an alcoholic. I have the double problem. I don't know why. I had fine folks, every opportunity. They did too much for me. My father was a very influential politician in New York. Any time I got in a scrape he got me out. I started drinking in grade school. I got in plenty of scrapes. My parents always shielded me. I was one of five boys. No girls. My parents thought the world of all of us. They gave us the best of everything. There was no dissension at home. We loved each other. A close Catholic family. I can't tell you why I was a drunk by the time I was 13.

I was in prep school, coming home from parties three in the morning, banging up cars, getting arrested and put in jail. Always my father got me out. This gave me a crutch.

I was a five-letter man at school and I was given the opportunity to go into professional football. I quit school and signed up. My parents had to sign because I was a minor.

The first week in training, living in a beautiful hotel, it cost $50 a day, I had the conveniences of all millionaires. I was invited out to a party and never returned to the hotel until about four in the morning, breaking one of the strictest rules they had in football. I crept up the back stairway, reached the fourth floor, and I slipped and fell, fell the four floors down the stairs. The noise was something, and next day I was brought before the manager and the owner of the club and really given a going over. I said it wouldn't happen again.

Somehow, it hurt my ego to have been talked to like that. Naturally, that called for action. I woke up six in the morning lying on the grass in back of the playing field. I had got drunk and blacked out. I was fired.

This started me on the nine year cross-country binge. I was hired and fired from teams. It seemed that every time I was fired there was a telegram waiting for me, inviting me to join another club. They thought they could dry me out, give me some guidance, and that would eventually

---

* Excerpted from David Dressler (ed.), *Readings in Criminology and Penology,* New York, N. Y.: Columbia Univ. Press, 1964.

net them a lot of money. I was always told I had ability, and I proved this on different occasions. I have been a national star, setting records that were reported in every paper in the United States. Once I won a game practically by myself. The funny thing was I was completely ignorant of the fact. I was loaded. Drunk.

I stayed with one club almost the whole season. Then I was fired. Again I'd broken training rules. I jumped on the train and went to Florida. I had a lot of money. I was paid off. Naturally, with big-shottitis, I went to the $50 a day hotel where I started, forgetting that back then the club was paying the freight. Carousing. Night clubs. Money ran short and I went to a middle class hotel. Then to a small hotel. Then to a room.

I finally started selling my wardrobe. Hocking my clothes. I finally wound up with one suit and a pair of bathing trunks.

I was really in the throes of alcoholism at that time. I had seen men living on the beach, so I sold my last suit and put on my trunks and went to live on the beach.

Now I was living on the beach. We were making it the best we could. One of the boys I hung around with came up with the idea that I'd been to a lot of fine houses where the ball team had been invited, that I'd know the layout of the houses, and would know how to break in and grab some liquor off. Or whatever we could use. Well, I didn't want to steal anything, but I would do anything to get that drink, so we broke into this home, and I knew exactly where they kept their liquor. We got away with this kind of thing for quite some time, but finally we were caught.

Again the long arm of politics, and again my crutch came to my rescue. I was given a lecture and told to go back to playing football. To quit drinking and behave myself.

By this time the war had started. Pearl Harbor was bombed. I was put in 3A.

Then I found that I had gone downtown with three other boys to enlist in the army. We all had been drinking. They were all single and in 1A. After the examinations we all met outside, waiting for the returns. All three of them had got turned down and I had been accepted.

I was shipped to the ETO [1] and eight months later I was hurt. They brought me back to the states in a semi-paralyzed condition and operated on my chest and took out two ribs that were paralyzing my nerves and stopping my head from going from side to side. This is where I was introduced to morphine and HMCs and I found this to be a great comfort. I became an addict at this time.

I was in the hospital for quite some time and all this time they gave me drugs to relieve the terrific pain that I had in the back of my head.

---

[1] European Theater of Operations.

That was what I wanted. Narcotics. After I got out of the hospital they gave me a letter to another one, where I reported to, and there I was given all the sedation and medication I needed. Between this and alcohol I soon became a raving maniac. I acquired five 502s [citations for drunk driving]. I was thrown into jails. I was handcuffed to the bars.

Drugs absolutely crazed me. I'd go days and not remember a thing. I don't remember trying to push my wife out of the automobile going at 90 miles an hour, and police chasing me. These were complete, total blackouts. I don't even remember the time my wife had to hide in the cement mixer for over five hours, where I had been stalking her like a lion with a big butcher knife. She said I tried to kill her.

Incidentally, my father passed away about this time. I knew I had lost my crutch. At this particular time something seemed to come into my mind. I knew this was going to wind up, this marriage, this way of life we were leading, me full of drugs, she drunk all the time. I had been given every opportunity in life, and here, right now, I knew I had lost my crutch, my father. From now on anything I would do, I was on my own. It seemed that the whole world had been taken away from me. I was full of nothing but utter despair, because now I knew this was the end.

Now understand. All this while I'm up to the ears in dope. I came upon the idea that I would take my last possession, my automobile, and I would sell it, and I would go to the race track at Delmar and make a lot of money. Then I would have money for my wife to live on, and I would take my discharge papers with me, and I would go on and end it some place in the world, which I didn't know and I didn't care, and the government would bury me. It seemed logical. I was hopped up, you understand.

I did this. I sold my car. I went to Delmar. And the first thing I did was register at the Delmar Hotel and get a $17 a day room. I got a cab and went out to the race track. I remember, when I got there, looking around for somebody to score off of.

Anyway, I awoke next morning at three in the morning, on the beach. I had paid $17 for a room, and here I wound up sleeping on the beach. The first thing, I reached into my pocket, and there, that horror, that feeling, that lost moment came upon me that I was penniless. I didn't have any money at all.

I picked myself up and went back into the room. I waited and found some friends of mine, borrowed a few dollars, got a fix, ran into another dear friend of mine, who gave me another fix and put me up for a week or so.

We went to Tijuana and brought back stuff. I was holed in somewhere I never saw the sun. Just fixing and sleeping and fixing.

People ask how people like us got started on drugs. We don't worry about that too much. We worry about staying clean a day at a time, not how we got addicted. After a time, though, we get to analyzing things. And I still don't know.

There was the fact my father was a crutch, always got me out of things. But over and above everything, all us alcoholics and narcotics are running away from something. That's why we drink, why we take drugs. What was I running from? I'm not sure. Maybe a hidden fear, of not being able to get to the top. My father was at the top, in politics. Always being put up for this office and that office. Me, I'd start at the top, time and again, and not quite make it.

A narcotic, a junkie, he builds up an expensive habit and he has to have the stuff. I never met a junkie that couldn't get what he needed. I've known some that had a $250 a day habit—I'm not kidding. Somehow, they got the money. You have to. You chisel, borrow, steal. Any addict will give another one just a little fix if he has anything extra, because someday he'll be hard up, he'll feel those grappling hooks in his stomach, and he wants to be able to get something from another addict.

An addict will arrive in a town he's never been in. He walks down the main stem, and in the hour he has scored. He has found a pusher. Don't ask me how they do it. They do.

These laws they're talking about, to give the death penalty to peddlers. That's nonsense. It won't get the big guys, the wholesalers, the importers, the smugglers. Know who'll get the gas chamber? The user. The junkie. Because more than likely he pushes on the side, to support his habit. He buys the stuff, cuts it down, sells part so he'll be able to have a fix tomorrow off the profits.

An addict will find somebody who doesn't use. He'll get him to chippy around until he's hooked. Now he has to have the stuff, he'll do anything for it. He buys from the junkie that started him off.

You would think all anyone would ever have to do to stay off drugs is just watch somebody kick it. The agony. The fits. The vomiting. The cramps. They go crazy. Every person I ever knew who got hooked wanted more than anything else in the world to quit. There's no enjoyment in using. The addict doesn't have beautiful dreams, so far as I ever could recall. All he has is sores all over his body, a running nose, and a pain in the belly. And still he'll use. That's what he means when he says, "I've got a monkey on my back." There's very few of us can shake that monkey off, believe me.

What Do You Think?

1.   Would you agree that it is nonsense to give the death penalty to peddlers? Why or why not?

2.   What would you suggest to help these kinds of individuals shake "the monkey" off their backs?

3.   What does this reading suggest as to the causes of drug usage?

7.   "ALL WE HAVE TO DO IS OPEN OUR MINDS " *

The Oracle *is an underground newspaper considered by many to speak for the "hippie" culture of San Francisco. The quotations below from an* Oracle *article suggests a direction in which many hippie leaders would like to go. What does this suggest as to the causes of drug usage?*

Today's headlines are often dominated by the so-called "Now Generation." Perhaps the most popularly used name for this group is "Hippie."

An important part of this new drug scene is the attempt by many of its adherents to adopt patterns of life radically different from traditional American modes of behavior. Many of these people, predominantly young, look to Oriental philosophy, Utopian ideals, and increased sensual experience. What is the nature of this movement? What are the ideals of these people? What significance can we attach to these developments? Why are people becoming attracted to a world which revolves around marijuana, methamphetamines, LSD, and other drugs?

Ganja is a very superior grade of Indian hemp much stronger than the best marijuana available in the United States. Allen Ginsberg was in India for a long while, and his *First Manifesto to End the Bringdown* is perhaps the best source of reasons [for] . . . marijuana smoking.

[The excerpts below extoll the spiritual "benefits" to be derived.]

A goodly number of us know this by the most directly convincing evidence possible. Speaking for many who are friends and for myself, I have not the slightest reservation in saying that this much maligned plant has powers that can elevate the human condition from a purely material plane to the spiritual. If this is opinion, it is the one shared with four hundred million others in the world. . . .

Awareness must expand from within each one of us. It is always there, in the void, this essence of what has been called the Divine. And all we have to do is open our minds and out it pours—whether through drugs or meditation, through love or fasting, music and dance or silence and quietude, its attainment is a reminder of the state of existence inside one's self-awareness that is fulfilled in itself, that underlies all being,

---

* Excerpted from R. Taini *et al., Drugs Among the Young,* Central City Multi-Service Center, 272 Sixth Street, San Francisco, California.

that is infinite joy and infinite love. It needs no future; it has assimilated the past; it lives in the present, bright and infinitely quiet. This is the state of expanded awareness to which all other sensitivity we hope leads. Where in the outer world do we find more than traces of the feeling except in fields and forests, or on oceans or mountain peaks? And why can't we match this inner reality with the outer, less flowing, less traceable world of the material? . . .

Inside this wall [a dead-layer in us] . . . we hide our secret feelings and our secret desires. The man-made world, it seems is a perfect model of this theorem. Our houses are collections of compartments, each containing its secret identifications and protecting its own areas of falsehood and fear. . . .

Our cities with their block lines and their property lines and their walls and their floors and their separations seem to be merely an extension ad infinitum of our unwillingness to accept our inner selves and, hence our unwillingness to accept each other. . . .

Why should we continue to live surrounded by feelingless objects, store-bought, anonymous, unresponsive to our own needs. In this new world nothing will be done that cannot be done with love and involvement, for the only drudges such a world can afford will be its machines. . . .

This will be a new age of craftsmanship, its appreciation of life processes expressed in its furniture, its clothing, dishware, and its utensils; and art, in the form of object, separate and distinct from the process of life, will have less and less meaning; for depth involvement in life will replace the watcher-listener mode of today. . . .

Along with renewed sense of the personal will come its counterpart, an increasing feeling of social oneness and universality, but no longer in the isolated terms of today, for as personalism increases, individualism, as we know it, will decrease. No longer will we consider ourselves as Mc-Luhan [1] does,—"Strangers in a world full of strangers." For we are not alone, and we never have been. We will learn to live in continuous and deep involvement with each other, and this open and transparent and interactive, where self-disclosure and acceptance are assumed as the basis of human growth.

What Do You Think?

1. What evidence is offered to support the contention that marihuana can "elevate the human condition from a purely material plane to the spiritual"?

---

[1] Marshall McLuhan, noted professor and author.

2.   The statement is made that "Awareness must expand from within each one of us." What besides drugs might help bring about such awareness?

8.   THE GENERATION GAP *

In this article, a sociologist suggests some reasons for the idealism-realism conflict between young and old. What might this have to do with drugs?

[Youth speaks, and age says, "This is nonsense, and when you grow up, you will be as we are." Realistically stated, today's wild young radical will most likely be tomorrow's suburban conservative.]

Though both youth and age claim to see the truth, the old are more conservatively realistic than the young, because on the one hand they take Utopian ideals less seriously and on the other hand take what may be called operating ideals, if not more seriously, at least more for granted. Thus, middle-aged people notoriously forget the poetic ideals of a new social order which they cherished when young. In their place, they put simply the working ideals current in the society. There is, in short, a persistent tendency for the ideology of a person as he grows older to gravitate more and more toward the status quo ideology, unless other facts (such as a social crisis or hypnotic suggestion) intervene. With advancing age, he becomes less and less bothered by inconsistencies in ideals. He tends to judge ideals according to whether they are widespread and hence effective in thinking about practical life, not according to whether they are logically consistent. Furthermore, he gradually ceases to bother about the untruth of his ideals, in the sense of their failure to correspond to reality. He assumes through long habit that, though they do not correspond perfectly, the discrepancy is not significant. The reality of an ideal is defined for him in terms of how many people accept it rather than how completely it is mirrored in actual behavior. Thus, we call him, as he approaches middle age, a realist.

The young, however, are idealist, partly because they take working ideals literally and partly because they acquire ideals not fully operative in the social organization. Those in authority over children are obligated as a requirement of their status to inculcate ideals as part of the official culture given the new generation. The children are receptive because they have little social experience—experience being systematically kept from

---

* Excerpted from Kingsley Davis, "The Sociology of Parent-Youth Conflict," *American Sociological Review*, 1940, as reprinted in Jerome Seidmon, (ed.), *The Adolescent: A Book of Readings*. New York, N. Y.: Henry Holt and Company, 1960.

them (by such means as censorship, for example, a large part of which is to "protect" children). Consequently, young people possess little ballast for their acquired ideals, which therefore soar to the sky, whereas the middle-aged, by contrast, have plenty of ballast.

This relatively unchecked idealism in youth is eventually complicated by the fact that young people possess keen reasoning ability. The mind simply as a logical machine, works as well at sixteen as at thirty-six.

Such logical capacity, combined with high ideals and an initial lack of experience, means that youth soon discovers with increasing age that the ideals it has been taught are true and consistent are not so in fact. Mental conflict thereupon ensues, for the young person has not learned that ideals may be useful without being true and consistent. As a solution, youth is likely to take action designed to remove inconsistencies or force actual conduct into line with ideals, such action assuming one of several typical adolescent forms—from religious withdrawal to the militant support of some Utopian scheme—but in any case consisting essentially in serious allegiance to one or more of the ideal moral systems present in the culture.

Some experts see the problem as one of a gap between young and old—the generation gap. A favorite slogan of youth seems to be "don't trust anyone over 30."

The adult clings to what he is accustomed, what was, what worked, what his life experience has proved valuable. Youth, responding to a new world, one in fantastic day-to-day change, with "instant news, instant music, and instant fun," used to watching fantastic events while they happen (instead of days or weeks afterward), *not* by second hand: youth has indeed developed a new perspective on life.

What Do You Think?

1. Would you agree that most adults today are "realists" while most young people are "idealists"?
2. Can the "generation gap" that the author identifies be bridged? If so, how?

9. WHY ARE SO MANY *NOT* USING DRUGS? *

There may be no trust by the young for those over 30, but certainly those over 30 have become deeply involved in the question of drug

---

* Excerpted from J. Fort, "Social Values, American Youth and Drug Use," paper presented at the National Association of Student Personnel Administrators' Drug Education Conference, Washington, D. C., November 7–8, 1966.

abuse. Dr. Joel Fort, consultant on drug abuse to the World Health Organization, comments:

Let us now look at the broader society. What is the great society that we all hear about, and where is it? Half of the American families are living in poverty; yet we are spending more than two billion dollars a month on a questionable war. We have vast slums. Crime is an enormous and growing problem. Our air and water are heavily polluted. Racial segregation, mental illness, sexual excesses of various kinds, family disruption, political extremism and accelerating bureaucracy and automation in American life are just some of the major social problems which provide *the foundation for the drug use which is occurring*. Philosophically, we should not only ask why so many are using drugs, but also why so many are not using them as we approach "1984."

If we see drug use as representing rebellion or protest, we must see it also as a reflection of apathy, overconformity, and acceptance of the status quo. Thoreau once said, "Most men lead lives of quiet desperation." It would be hard to prove that the situation has changed since those times, except for the desperation becoming noisier. He also made a very profound observation that is quite pertinent to our discussion when he said "There are a thousand people hacking away at the branches of evil for every one striking at the roots."

We really have two co-existing problems. Campus life shows a massive degree of apathy and other-directed conformity combined with some nonconformity, dissent, and illicit drug use, including alcohol, marijuana and LSD.

We should also think of the words of the recent folk-rock tunes as they reflect the thinking of our youth. "Nowhere," "Little Boxes," and "The Eve of Destruction" were three of the most popular. All of you have seen some of the badges that people are wearing as signs of their protests. Two of the most popular are a picture of Adolph Eichmann with the caption, "I Was Only Doing My Job," and one which says, "I Am a Human Being. Do Not Fold, Spindle, or Mutilate."

What Do You Think?

1. Do men today still "lead lives of quiet desperation"? Explain.
2. Fort suggests that American society as a whole provides the foundation for the drug use which is occurring. What does he mean? Would you agree? Why or why not?

10. THE CHRONIC DRUG USER

The potential for turning to a life of constant drug use has been a major concern of the people considering the drug problem in our country. Few would deny that there are chronic drug users. But what causes them to turn to long-term drug use? The next three excerpts present examples of chronic drug users. What factors brought about such drug usage on their part?

[The story of a young woman long addicted to drugs:]

I came from an upper middle class family that was held together by money and hypocrisy. Forget love for that is an unknown quality in my family. I was made to understand that it was my fault for everything that went wrong in my house for not being the perfect child they had wanted in the first place. As a result the only thing I could readily expect were beatings and the constant reiterating that I wasn't good enough. When I was seventeen years of age I went to live in a foster home. It was a nice home but it was unsuccessful because to put it mildly, I was an emotional wreck. When your mother continuously says you are a mess I can guarantee that you will eventually become one. Because of this mess I had my first nervous breakdown and I was told by the "shrinks" [psychiatrists] in the hospital that my mother was harming me beyond repair. I was in the hospital almost four months on heavy medication. When I came out I was an addict, completely dependent on pills. Pills can do a lot for you. They enable you to continue living when you don't want to. They dull the deep hurts that have ripped you apart time and time again by society and individuals. I was lucky because I could keep saying that I had lost my prescriptions in order to support my habit. I had to use the hospital pharmacy because if I didn't, I would be forced to get them elsewhere and really wouldn't be sure of what I would be getting, which would be more harmful to me than the pills. Unfortunately it wasn't long before the hospital medications became inadequate for meeting my craving. I graduated to other pills and barbiturates such as phenobarbital.

[A chronic narcotic addict expresses his views:]

I have been using hard narcotics or I have been a "hype" for a couple of years. Every now and then I would get a large supply of heroin or some other opiate and I would allow myself a binge of up to two weeks but no more. At the end of two weeks I would have a minor yen going and I would stop the run. Also, I would break up the opiate run with stimulants (methedrine, etc.) which would "burn" the opiates

out of my system. I would take these precautions against becoming addicted because I wanted to be of this world. I wanted to keep myself
free to seek a direction for myself in a world that I felt was possibly
worthy of a person's participation in it. But I lost faith in the few
causes I had continued to believe in. I quit being a spectator, that is
watching other addicts and trying to help them and decided to be an
addict. No more ambition to change the world or try to save the world,
no more dreams about being or becoming equipped to help others, no
more wondering what path to take to help people the most. When I woke
up in the morning I knew what I wanted. I had a focal point to live around.
When I went to bed I knew whether or not I had had a successful day.
No question about what I wanted to be. I had a Ph.D. in drug addiction.[1]

[Other drugs and other situations suggest other causes for the chronic
use of drugs:]

There's John, a quiet one, 31 and the only Negro in the group. He
just flipped out on pain-killing Demerol tablets after stomach surgery in
a hospital; later he started taking methedrine by mouth, shifted to the
needle, and became a confirmed crystal shooter. . . .

There's Betty, a motherly 46 year old with 20 years of alcoholism and
a long mental hospital record behind her. Trapped years ago by the
amphetamines in easily available diet pills, she is one of the rare meth
users who never injected the drug. Popping pills has kept her high
enough.[2]

What Do You Think?

All of these accounts depict drug abuse of one sort or another
and in many varied situations. In what ways are they similar?
Different? How would you account for these similarities and
differences?

11. DRUGS AND RELIGION *

*There are at least four churches in existence in the United States
today that utilize psychedelic drugs as part of their sacrament. Here*

---

[1] Excerpted from *Drugs in the Tenderloin,* Central City Multi-Service Center,
272 Sixth Street, San Francisco, California, 1967.
[2] Excerpted from David Perlman, *San Francisco Chronicle,* December 7, 1967.
* Excerpted from W. N. Pahnke, "LSD and Religious Experience," reprinted in
Richard C. DeBold and R. C. Leaf, eds., *LSD, Man and Society.* Middletown,
Conn.: Wesleyan Univ. Press, 1967. Copyright © 1967 Wesleyan University
Press. Used by permission Wesleyan University Press.

is the statement of a divinity student who used a psychedelic compound, psilocybin:

Now four days after the experience itself I continued to feel a deep sense of awe and reverence being simultaneously intoxicated with an ecstatic joy. This euphoric feeling included elements of profound peace and steadfastness surging like a spring from the depth of my being which has rarely, if ever, been tapped prior to the drug experience. The spasmodic nature of my prayer life had ceased and I have yielded to a new need to spend time each day in meditation, which though essentially open and wordless, is impregnated by feelings of thanksgiving and trust. This increased need to be alone is balanced by what I believe to be a greater sensitivity to the authentic problems of others and a corresponding willingness to enter freely into genuine friendships. I possessed a renewed and increased sense of personal integration and am more content to be myself than previously. The feeling I experienced could best be described as cosmic tenderness, infinite love, penetrating peace, eternal blessing and unconditional acceptance on the one hand and on the other unspeakable awe, overflowing joy, primeval humility, inexpressible gratitude and boundless devotion. Yet all of these words are hopelessly inadequate and can do little more than meekly point towards the genuine, inexpressible feelings actually experienced. During the height of the experience I had no consciousness of time and space in the ordinary sense. I felt as though I was beyond seconds, minutes, hours, and also beyond past, present and future. In religious language I was in eternity. In no sense have I an urge to formulate philosophical or theological dogmas about my experience. Only my silence can retain its purity and genuineness.

What Do You Think?

Does this passage suggest a motivation for drug use that might also apply in other situations? Explain.

12. FACTORS IN THE DEVELOPMENT OF DRUG ABUSE *

Lastly, here is part of a report by the head of the Drug Abuse Information Project of the State of California.

The properties of the drug are of obvious importance in the development of a pattern of drug misuse, yet the use of a particular drug is not uniformly distributed through our society. This suggests that some groups

---

* Annual Report, State of California, Drug Abuse Information Project, 1967–68.

and certain individuals are more susceptible than others. In order to understand the development of the several different patterns of drug misuse one must consider three factors or influences:

A. Drug factors: The pharmacological effects of a drug are of great importance in determining its potential for misuse. Drugs that are commonly misused are quite different and indeed the effects of one group may be diametrically opposed to those of another group of misused drugs. For each drug or drug class the hazard to the user and to society must be evaluated. This evaluation will be quite different for different drugs.

B. Individual Psychological Factors: Drug misuse does not reflect simply the availability of the drug. Additional factors must be operating to determine individual liability. Alcohol, the most commonly misused drug, is freely available to all members of our culture but our patterns of alcohol use vary widely. Some individuals reject it, some use it temperately and socially, some use it episodically to excess and a tragically large number develop a compulsive pattern of misuse which destroys their own and other lives.

C. Group Sociological Factors: Individuals form attitudes and react as members of groups. The attitudes and problems of their group condition their use of drugs. Heroin misuse, now declining in incidence, was predominantly a disease or crime of the ghettos of large cities. Other ethnic or religious groups in our society are statistically unusually susceptible or resistant to development of chronic alcoholism.

The attitudes of the dominant group in our culture are reflected in the laws such as those that are permissive of alcohol, tobacco and other social recreational drugs, which are actually quite harmful. There are, of course, sub-groups within our pluralistic society which feel the prohibitions against their social drugs are arbitrary and unjustified by action of the drugs. This conflict between groups is the basis for the current criticism of laws regulating the use of marihuana.

What Do You Think?

Compare the factors cited in this article with many of the causes suggested by the other readings in this chapter. Do they reinforce each other? How are they different? How would you explain any differences that you noticed?

ACTIVITIES FOR INVOLVEMENT

1. Invite a qualified opponent of contemporary drug use to speak to your class. Present him with a number of the reasons for drug use suggested in this chapter and ask him to react. Then ask him to explain his position. What evidence can he offer to support his views?

2.   Frequently the phrase "they feel" or "they say" prefaces remarks made about controversial issues. Admittedly it is the feelings of people that eventually decide what the opinion of a given culture or society will be on a given subject. Conduct an informal survey to determine what the attitude in your school and community is towards drug use. Notice especially (take notes) of how people respond to the word "drugs" itself (no matter what they might know about the issue). Then hold a class discussion on whether the word "drugs" affects people more than other key words in our culture such as "liquor," "sex," or "racist."

3.   Some people have suggested that widespread drug use among high school students has nothing to do with the social situation of the users. These people have then concluded that there is something elementally *wrong* with our society—something that is not the unique problem of one group or another. Suppose that you were asked to rebut or support this position. What would you say? Present your arguments to the class. What counter-arguments can they offer?

4.   Review all of the readings in this chapter. Then list all of the reasons that you can think of which contribute to teen-age drug use. Then rank these factors in order from most to least serious. Compare your list with those made by your classmates. Defend your ranking, but then discuss: Is there *one most serious* cause for drug usage among teens? Be prepared to explain your reasoning.

5.   How do you suppose that a visitor from another country would explain why Americans use drugs? Write a short statement in which you express what you think he might say.

6.   A college professor in California conducted an informal survey using a very small sample, in which he asked people why they *started* using drugs. The responses that he obtained are as follows (not in order of frequency of response):

Curiosity.

"Going along with the gang."

Afraid of being left out.

Desired to.

No good reason for not doing so, so decided to try it.

Forced to do so by peers.

Medical reasons.

For "kicks."

Which of these, if any, do you think is the most adequate explanation for *starting* to use drugs? If you feel that none of these reasons is adequate, what explanation(s) would you offer?

5

Opinions About Drug Usage

What should be done about drugs? Any controversial issue—and the use of drugs is certainly a controversial issue in American society today—arouses a number of opinions. When we look at the wide variety of conflicting views that have been formed about drugs by various groups and individuals, it soon becomes evident that people are considerably divided in their feelings about drug use —and abuse. This chapter presents a number of these diverse, and often conflicting, viewpoints. What do you think should be done?

1. "DO WE OR DON'T WE WANT INDIVIDUALS SMOKING MARIHUANA?" *

A California physician presents his views on the use of marihuana:

THE CURRENT PROBLEM

In effect the problem today is, Do we or don't we want individuals smoking marihuana? Some sociologists argue that "since smoking marihuana will undoubtedly continue regardless of legislation against it, it can also be argued that it would be better to accept the inevitable than to wage war for a lost cause." And some also argue that we should treat the marihuana problem the same as we have the alcohol problem. The difficulty, however, is that we have never really managed the alcohol problem; the abusive use of alcohol has created the major drug problem in the United States today.

---

* Excerpted from E. R. Bloomguist, "Marihuana: Social Benefit or Social Detriment?" *California Medicine* 106:352, 1967.

Certainly there is wisdom in the comment of the President's Ad Hoc Panel on Drug Abuse: "It is the opinion of the Panel that the hazards of marihuana per se have been exaggerated and that long criminal sentences imposed on an occasional user or possessor of the drug are in poor social perspective." But before transcending the meaning of this recommendation and permitting all who might wish to use marihuana to do so, it would be well to recall the warning of this country's sixteenth President who held that destruction of our nation could not come from abroad, but "If destruction be our lot, we ourselves must be its author and finisher. As a nation of free men, we must live through all time, or die by suicide."

Although President Lincoln had no reference to drug abuse when he made this statement, he could not have painted a clearer picture of a national menace where drug abuse is concerned.

What Do You Think?

How do you suppose those in favor of drug use might respond to this argument? How would those who oppose drug use respond?

2. AN A.M.A. "WHITE PAPER" *

The following study was released by the American Medical Association and the National Research Council in 1968.

After careful appraisal of available information concerning marihuana (cannabis) and its components, the Council on Mental Health and the Committee on Alcoholism and Drug Dependence of the American Medical Association and the Committee on Problems of Drug Dependence of the National Research Council, National Academy of Sciences, reached the following conclusions:

1. *Cannabis is a dangerous drug and as such is a public health concern.*

For centuries, the hemp plant (cannabis) has been used extensively and in various forms as an intoxicant in Asia, Africa, South America, and elsewhere. With few exceptions, organized societies consider such

---

* "Marihuana and Society—Council on Mental Health and the Committee on Alcoholism and Drug Dependence of the A. M. A. and the Committee on Problems of Drug Dependence of the National Research Council, National Academy of Science," *The Journal of the American Medical Association* 204:91, 1968.

use undesirable and therefore a drug problem, and have imposed legal and social sanctions on the user and the distributor.

Some of the components of the natural resins obtained from the hemp plant are powerful psychoactive agents; hence the resins themselves may be. In dogs and monkeys, they have produced complete anesthesia of several days' duration with quantities of less than 10 mg/kg.

Although dose-response curves are not so accurately defined in man, the orders of potency on a weight (milligram) basis are greater than those for many other powerful psychoactive agents, such as the barbiturates. They are markedly greater than those for alcohol. In India, where weak decoctions are used as a beverage, the government prohibits charas, the potent resin, even for use in folk medicine. In many countries where chronic heavy use of cannabis occurs, such as Egypt, Morocco, and Algeria, it has a marked effect of reducing the social productivity of a significant number of persons.

The fact that no physical dependence develops with cannabis does not mean it is an innocuous drug. Many stimulants are dangerous psychoactive substances although they do not cause physical dependence.

2. *Legalization of marihuana would create a serious abuse problem in the United States.*

The current use of cannabis in the United States contrasts sharply with its use in other parts of the world. In this country, the pattern of use is primarily intermittent and of the "spree" type, and much of it consists of experimentation by teenagers and young adults. Further, hemp grown in the United States is not commonly of high potency and "street" samples sometimes are heavily adulterated with inert materials.

With intermittent and casual use of comparatively weak preparations, the medical hazard is not so great, although even such use when it produces intoxication can give rise to disorders of behavior with serious consequences to the individual and to society.

And, while it is true that now only a small proportion of marihuana users in the United States are chronic users and can be said to be strongly psychologically dependent on the drug, their numbers, both actual and potential, are large enough to be of public health concern.

If all controls on marihuana were eliminated, potent preparations probably would dominate the legal market, even as they are now beginning to appear on the illicit market. If the potency of the drug were legally controlled, predictably there would be a market for the more powerful illegal forms.

When advocates of legalizing marihuana claim that it is less harmful than alcohol, they are actually comparing the relatively insignificant effects of marihuana at the lower end of the dose-response curve with the effects of alcohol at the toxicity end of the curve—ie, the "spree" use of marihuana vs acute or chronic "poisoning" with alcohol. If they compared both drugs at the upper end of the curve, they would see that the effects on the individual and society are highly deleterious in both cases.

Admittedly, if alcohol could be removed from the reach of alcoholics, one of the larger medical and social problems could be solved. But to make the active preparations of cannabis generally available would solve nothing. Instead, it would create a comparable problem of major proportions.

That some marihuana users are now psychologically dependent, that nearly all users become intoxicated, and that more potent forms of cannabis could lead to even more serious medical and social consequences—these facts argue for the retention of legal sanctions.

3. *Penalties for violations of the marihuana laws are often harsh and unrealistic.*

Persons violating federal law with respect to possession of marihuana are subject to penalties of from 2 to 10 years imprisonment for the first offense, 5 to 20 years for the second offense, and 10 to 40 years for additional offenses. Suspension of sentence, probation, and parole are allowed only for the first offense. Many of the state laws provide for comparable penalties. With respect to sale, penalties are even more severe.

Laws should provide for penalties in such a fashion that the courts would have sufficient discretion to enable them to deal flexibly with violators. There are various degrees of both possession and sale. Possession ranges from the youngster who has one or two marihuana cigarettes to an individual who has a substantial quantity. Sale may range from the transfer of a single cigarette to the disposition of several kilograms of the drug.

While persons should not be allowed to become involved with marihuana with impunity, legislators, law enforcement officials, and the courts should differentiate in the handling of the occasional user, the chronic user, the person sharing his drug with another, and the dealer who sells for a profit.

Of particular concern is the youthful experimenter who, by incurring a criminal record through a single thoughtless act, places his future career in jeopardy. The lives of many young people are being needlessly damaged.

For those persons who are chronic users of the drug, and are psychologically dependent on it, general medical and psychiatric treatment, plus social rehabilitative services, should be made readily available. Such persons should not be treated punitively for their drug abuse alone any more than are persons dependent on other drugs, such as narcotics or alcohol.

Furthermore, if the purpose of imposing penalties is to deter acts which might injure the individual and disrupt society, then equitable penalties, insofar as they enhance respect for the law, can contribute to effective prevention.

   4.   *Additional research on marihuana should be encouraged.*

Only recently has an active hallucinogenic principle of cannabis been exactly identified and synthesized. Sufficient time has not elapsed to obtain a substantial body of pharmacologic and clinical evidence concerning its effects. There are no carefully controlled clinical studies of long-time effects of cannabis on the central nervous or other organ systems. These and other considerations point to the importance of on-going research in this area.

It must be emphasized, however, that the issue which faces the United States today is not whether we know all there is to know about marihuana scientifically. Obviously every effort should be made to correct the deficiencies in our knowledge. The issue is whether we can ignore the experiences and observations established over centuries of heavy use of hemp preparations in various societies. A current solution to the problem does not relate to what is not known, but to those facts which are known about cannabis and its preparations. There is extensive experience in its use in all of its forms, including the effects of the potent natural resins which contain the active biological principles.

   5.   *Educational programs with respect to marihuana should be directed to all segments of the population.*

Educational material, based on scientific knowledge, should point out the nature of marihuana and the effects of its use. Such material should be an integral part of a total educational program on drug abuse.

Primary and secondary schools, as well as colleges and universities, should establish such programs.

The communications media should disseminate authoritative information to the general public.

Physicians, as professional practitioners and concerned members of the community, should call attention frequently and forcibly to the problems of drug abuse and drug dependence.

An informed citizenry, in the final analysis, is the most effective deterrent of all.

What Do You Think?

   1.   What does the A. M. A. mean when they state "in the final analysis, an informed citizenry is the most effective deterrent of all"?

   2.   Which A. M. A. conclusion seems strongest? Weakest? Explain your reasoning.

3. SHOULD THE USE OF MARIHUANA BE LEGALIZED?

*Students, hippies, some responsible medical authorities, and some edu-
cators strongly support either legalization of marihuana or significant
reduction in the penalties associated with the possession and consumption of the drug.*

A Statement by Allen Ginsberg *

I believe that future generations will have to rely on new faculties
of awareness, rather than new versions of old idea-systems, to cope with the
increasing godlike complexity of our planetary civilization, with its over-
population, its threat of atomic annihilation, its centralized network of
abstract word-image communications, its power to leave earth. A new
consciousness, or new awareness, will evolve to meet a changed ecological
environment. It has already begun evolving in younger generations from
Prague to Calcutta; part of the process of re-examination of certain
heretofore discarded "primitive" devices of communication with Self
and Selves. Negro worship rituals have invaded the West via New Orleans
and Liverpool, in altered but still recognizably functional form. The
consciousness-expanding drugs (psychedelics) occupy attention in the
highest intellectual circles of the West, as well as among a great mass
of youth. The odd perceptions of Zen, Tibetan Yoga, Mantra Yoga, and
indigenous American shamanism affect the consciousness of a universal
generation, children who can recognize each other by hairstyle, tone of
voice, attitude to nature and attitude to Civilization. The airwaves are
filled with songs of hitherto unheard-of frankness and beauty.

These then are some of the political or social implications of the
legalization of marihuana as a catalyst to self-awareness. The generaliza-
tions I have made may also apply to the deeper affects [1] and deeper
social changes that may be catalyzed thru the already massive use
of psychedelic drugs.

White House Conference on Narcotic and Drug Abuse *

It is the opinion of the Panel that the hazards of Marihuana per se
have been exaggerated and that long criminal sentences imposed on an

---

* Excerpted from Allen Ginsberg, "First Manifesto to End the Bringdown," in
The Marihuana Papers, David Solomon (ed.). Indianapolis, Ind.: The Bobbs-
Merrill Company, Inc., 1966.
[1] Emotions or feelings.
* Excerpted from Proceedings White House Conference on Narcotic and Drug
Abuse, September 27–28, 1962, State Department Auditorium, Washington, D. C.

occasional user or possessor of the drug are in poor social perspective. Although Marihuana has long held the reputation of inciting individuals to commit sexual offenses and other antisocial acts, the evidence is inadequate to substantiate this. Tolerance and physical dependence do not develop and withdrawal does not produce an abstinence syndrome.

What Do You Think?

1.   How might the A. M. A. respond to Ginsberg's position? What arguments could they use?
2.   Should the penalties for marihuana use be lessened? Give your reasons.

4.   DOES IT TAKE AN ACID HEAD TO TREAT ONE? *

Should doctors take drugs? Scientists disagree as to the value of trying LSD themselves in order to become more effective in treating their patients who are drug users:

In a tenement in New York's East Village, the hippies and flower children lie draped on chairs and sprawled over the floor. If some are on LSD trips, it is difficult to discern. The herbal scent of marijuana is strong in the room. One fashionably bearded and dirty young hippie speaks out: "I can't trip out because I sense a bad voyage, and my shrink's over there in the corner on a trip of his own." A pretty girl, looking like Eliza Doolittle before Professor Higgins encouraged her to bathe, kindly interprets: "He thinks LSD will have a bad effect on him this time. His psychiatrist is also on a trip and will be unavailable to help him."

The "psychiatrist" in the corner is not a physician at all. He is another hippie, a college dropout. If the love generation was having some fun with the squares in the room, all was not flower children mockery.

Some psychiatrists and behavioral therapists have been taking LSD because they believe that they will have a greater understanding of what the victims of LSD-induced psychoses go through. Sharing this view is Dr. Victor Gioscia, associate professor of sociology and philosophy at New York's Adelphi University and a consultant for the Joint Commission on the Mental Health of Children. He told a meeting of the American

---

* "Does It Take an Acid Head to Treat One?" *Medical World News,* March 22, 1968. Copyright © 1968 McGraw-Hill, Inc.

Orthopsychiatric Association in Chicago this week that his study of LSD users and their therapists in New York, San Francisco, and London indicates that acid heads more easily accept a therapist who has taken LSD.

A ROUTE TO EMPATHY

The concept that it takes one to treat one is unorthodox and highly controversial, but Dr. Gioscia feels that a therapist who has not taken LSD faces a number of problems in trying to treat hippies. They regard him as ignorant, square, mercenary, and puritanical. And the therapist feels limited in his ability to empathize with the hippies and their LSD experiences.

The therapist who has taken LSD "will know how to talk his patient down," says the New York sociologist. But a therapist who has not experienced an LSD trip usually does not know that "a patient in a bad trip can be talked down," and so he resorts to medication, which can create other problems because the drugs given may produce adverse effects in a patient who has taken a hallucinogen.

Many therapists surveyed by Dr. Gioscia said that they would like to try LSD but that legal considerations prevented them. "Some therapists thought they would eventually try it."

If some therapists are becoming part of the acid scene in order to help patients, the psychiatrists interviewed by MWN strongly oppose the practice. "You don't let a rattlesnake bite you to find out if you're immune," says Dr. Jules H. Masserman, professor of neurology and psychiatry at Northwestern University, who was one of the first psychiatrists to study the possible use of LSD in treating mental disorders.

"Taking LSD can only make the therapist more wary of the dangers inherent in the drug," Dr. Masserman stresses. "There is an easier, safer, and in my opinion more practical way for the therapist to learn. There is sufficient literature, patient analysis, and other opportunities available to the psychiatrist to learn the ins and outs of drug usage without endangering his own mental and physical state. To say that a psychiatrist who spends years acquiring the knowledge to treat mental ills should join the hippies is out-and-out lunacy."

Another psychiatrist who feels strongly that a doctor's place is not in his patient's shoes is Dr. Daniel X. Freedman, chairman of the department of psychiatry at the University of Chicago. "Medical schools spend years trying to teach the fledgling therapist the dangers of over-identification. One of the biggest problems is training the psychiatry student to develop not only empathy but objectivity. Taking the drug with the intent of getting closer to the patient's viewpoint defeats all the schooling and can often result in two patients for the price of one."

THERAPISTS TAKE A TRIP

A Detroit psychotherapist who admits that he has taken LSD agrees. "It was a frightening experience, and I found it absolutely no help in dealing with my patient's experiences. His reactions were entirely different from mine."

And a psychiatrist in San Francisco who went on a trip says: "I took LSD to experience it. I had what the hippies call a good trip. But I did not learn anything that would help me understand what happens to a patient on a bad trip. Now, when one of my patients is having a bad trip, I don't try to bring him down with chemicals—but not because I believe they cannot help. I prefer letting the patient know that I am with him and will help him over the rough spots."

It is generally agreed that each patient responds differently to drugs. "Our physical and mental make-up is such that no two people will experience the same effects," says Northwestern's Dr. Masserman. "Similarly, treatment of a bad trip depends on the individual."

Because the effects of LSD are unpredictable, most psychiatrists, like Dr. Masserman, insist that they need to know more about the drug. "But in order to understand the patient's separateness, we must maintain our own separateness."

What Do You Think?

Most psychiatrists seem to agree that they need to know more about LSD, but seem divided as to the best way to acquire such knowledge. Do you think the possible understanding gained from taking the drug would be worth the risks?

5.   THE WHOLE SCENE WILL GO UNDERGROUND *

In this reading a psychologist argues that it is impossible for a government to get people to stop using drugs if they don't want to.

It seems to me that the government is going ahead just really ignoring the fact that the primary use of psychedelics, whether by a 15 year old or a 50 year old, is either for the purposes of religion, creativity, self-behavior change or self-education. In some sense or other, and with

---

* Excerpted from R. Alpert, "A Symposium—Psychedelic Drugs and The Law," *Journal of Psychedelic Drugs* 1:24, 1967.

all of these motivations, goes an internal feeling of the righteousness of one's acts, and it is such righteousness that makes it impossible for a government to play upon feelings internal to people that would get them to want to stop. So that with this continuation, this increase in use, and as the penalties get higher and the undercover agents get better, the whole scene will go underground more and also many of us will go to jail. Most important, I think of what our reaction will be to increased pressure and increased legislation against psychedelics without any recognition of these positive uses.

What Do You Think?

1. The author states that it is a feeling of "internal righteousness" that makes it impossible for a government to get people to want to stop using drugs. What does this mean? Would you agree or not? Explain.

2. What does the author mean when he states that "the whole scene will go underground"? Can this be prevented?

6. A RISK OF PSYCHOTIC BREAKDOWN *

The California Medical Association argues that the medical evidence is clear: LSD use may bring about long-run physiological damage.

Marihuana does not produce physical addiction but it does produce significant dependence to a serious degree. This is a fact well known to doctors working with college students. The social influence surrounding the use of marihuana also encourages experimentation with other drugs, notably LSD and, of course, may lead into addiction to narcotics. We know now that long-term subtle psychologic damage may result from LSD. Such damage may be glossed over by the pleasure and enthusiasm engendered by the substance, but we have seen too many cases of psychic breakdown to doubt the serious danger of the drug. It is even possible that the brain is structurally damaged. There is recent evidence that LSD attacks hereditary genes. In short, our professional medical opinion is that playing with LSD is a desperately dangerous form of drug roulette. The medical evidence is clear; any person taking

---

* Excerpted from *Narcotics Inquiry Report,* San Mateo County (California) Juvenile Justice Commission, November, 1967. Quoted from a statement by the California Medical Association.

LSD runs the clear risk of psychotic breakdown and long-run physiological damage.

What Do You Think?

What impact might a message such as this from an organization of physicians have on people? What kind of reactions might be produced?

7. ACT NOW, THINK LATER *

A California social scientist argues for restraint rather than a headlong rush into legislation. Do his arguments seem reasonable?

A highly predictable response to social problems in the United States is legal repression, and this is doubly so when the threat involves non-medical use of unfamiliar drugs. The rapidly expanding use of LSD is currently triggering this response in various state legislatures throughout the country, whereas the Federal law makers are exercising considerable restraint. Their counterparts at the state level are rushing through punitive laws on the basis of instinct rather than reason. . . .

The . . . act-now-think-later approach to LSD legislation is occurring in several . . . states. . . .

How does one go about a rational appraisal of the non-medical uses of hallucinogens? First of all, it is helpful if we temporarily shelve the attitudinal stereotypes attached to non-medical drug use; otherwise, we are immediately involved in logical inconsistencies with regard to those culturally approved drugs, alcohol and tobacco. The social implications are then determined by 1) the effects of hallucinogenic drugs and 2) the number of persons who will use them in various degrees. . . .

My argument is that the majority of those who continue to use hallucinogens will attribute their motivations to lasting, as well as to immediate, effects.

Keeping this feature of the drug in mind, we can make some rational predictions about who will use hallucinogens, that is, who will be attracted by their capacity for influencing attitudes, beliefs and values. By far, the most important variable is age. The hallucinogens are effective modifiers of personality only if a person is seeking such a change or is at least open to it. . . . The less strongly a person is already

---

* Excerpted from W. H. McGlothlin, "Toward A Rational View of Hallucinogenic Drugs." *Journal of Psychedelic Drugs* 1:40–45, 1967.

committed to a set of beliefs, values, and goals, the more likely he is to accept as valid those he finds via the drug experience.

By the same reasoning, adults who are drawn to hallucinogenic drugs are likely to be those who, for one reason or another, find themselves alienated from the mainstream of culture. They spurn many of the commonplace gratifications society offers; they are often strongly interested in extrasensory perception and other pararational areas and generally turn inward in search of more meaningful existence. Highly structured, practical, conforming, outward people are very unlikely to be attracted to hallucinogenic drugs. Experimental evidence has shown that such people tend to be unwilling to try the drugs, respond very minimally, if they do participate, and do not report any lasting effects from the experience. Many LSD enthusiasts are unaware of these limitations. They correctly observe that their most vocal critics have never taken LSD, but rather naively believe that everyone would concur as to the benefits if they would only try it.

Given that we can say something about who will be attracted to hallucinogenic drugs, what are the effects of repeated use, especially the social implications? While there is considerable individual variation, the most consistent personal pattern is a lessening of concern over status, competition, material possessions and other pursuits of the achievement-oriented society in which we live. The LSD user often describes himself as more soft, loving and tolerant with less aggression, egocentrism and anxiety. He believes LSD has made him more accepting of himself and others; less prone to make one-sided judgments in terms of good and bad, right and wrong; and less prone to be assertive or make a strong commitment to cultural ideologies for which he himself sees no valid reason. . . .

Unfortunately, . . . LSD-induced wisdom is not accompanied by solutions for some of the basic demands of reality. He [the user] belongs to what Kenniston, in his book *The Uncommitted,* calls the "cult of the present." Totally absorbed with intensifying today's experience, he avoids thinking about the future, including basic economic realities. If pressed for his reasoning, in this regard, he will provide rather childlike rationalizations concerning the futility of planning in an atomic age or perhaps a belief that automation will somehow solve the world's economic problems. He may comfort himself with a vague, intuitive feeling that the world is about to metamorphose suddenly into a non-competitive, peaceful and benevolent utopia all by itself with no need for active intervention by himself or others. In short, he refuses responsibility both for his own self-direction and as contributor to the existing social order.

What Do You Think?

1. Can legislation stop drug usage?
2. The author urges a rational appraisal of the nonmedical uses of hallucinogens. Does he accomplish this in his own analysis? Explain.

ACTIVITIES FOR INVOLVEMENT

1. Some people have suggested that there is such a thing as a "drug type." Would you agree? Write a "Letter to the Editor" of an imaginary newspaper, in which you respond to this view. Be sure that you explain your reasoning clearly and carefully.

2. Hold a mock "Meet the Press" program in which one member of the class portrays a *non*-user explaining why he does *not* use drugs. The remainder of the class can then represent reporters from various newspapers questioning him.

3. Invite some members of your community (e.g., a minister, a housewife, a policeman, a social worker, a city councilman, a school dropout, etc.) to express their views on the role of drugs in American society today. Prepare questions (like the following) ahead of time to ask the speakers:
   a. How extensive do you believe drug usage is in our community? What evidence can you offer in support of your beliefs?
   b. What factors in the community might be contributing to drug use and abuse?
   c. What might we do to reduce or control drug usage?
Compare their responses with the views of the class on the same questions.

4. Many drug advocates argue that they get "turned on" by drugs. What do you think they mean? Listed below are a number of other ways that people have suggested one can get "turned on."
   By one's work.
   By having a lot of money.
   By one's religious beliefs.
   By being popular.
   Through being in love.
   Through exercising power over others.
   Through physical activity.
Add any additional possibilities that you can think of and then rank these reasons from one (1), lowest, to eight (8), highest. Explain why you ranked them as you did, and then compare your rankings with those of your classmates. Then hold a class discussion as to the most effective way to get more people "turned on" in a positive way.

5. Invite a physician to speak to the class on the use and abuse of drugs. Ask him to give his views on whether doctors who have tried drugs

themselves are able to treat more effectively their patients who are drug users. What evidence can he offer to support his opinions?

6.   Many people have suggested that drug use by teen-agers today is a form of "protest." Often you will hear people remark that there is a considerable amount of protest in our society these days. Listed below are a number of different kinds of protest that have been in evidence in recent times:

Student revolts at a number of colleges and universities.

Hunger strikes by prisoners.

Sit-ins by civil rights workers.

Picketing by union members.

Peace marches by anti-war groups.

Long hair and distinctive styles of dress among young people.

Would you agree that each of the above represent forms of protest today? Should drug usage be included? Why or why not? Do any of the above have anything in common with drug use? Explain.

7.   Many people argue that drug use (except under the prescription of a qualified physician) is dangerous to one's health and can affect the health of one's unborn children. Yet some religious sects believe that drugs are an important part of their ritual. In such cases, if a deformed child is born to a mother who has been using drugs, should the mother be exempt from any moral sanction since the argument could be made that she comes under the "freedom of religion" clause of the First Amendment to the U. S. Constitution? Explain your reasoning.

What Should Be Done?

6

What should be done about drug use and abuse? A number of "cures" and solutions have been proposed but none have received wide support. This chapter presents a number of readings which indicate some things that are currently being done, as well as some suggestions as to what might be tried. Which sounds most promising, and why?

1. HOW TO CURE A DRUG ADDICT *

Can addicts be cured? Here is a vivid description of what it means to try and break the heroin habit:

We got shots four times a day and an additional barbiturate sedative at night. They gave us a synthetic horror called Dolophine, which was invented in Germany under the Nazis and named after the great Adolf! The ward physician, another polite and good-natured young man, who visited us every morning, told me that it was easier to get off Dolophine than regular opiates. I'm sure that he was convinced of it. Everybody not addicted to drugs was convinced of it.

Day by day my dosages were decreased. I felt real discomfort and anxiety only about half an hour before each shot was administered. Sometimes the hack was late in dealing out the medications and this caused real suffering—pain in the knee joints, eyes out of focus, shortness of breath, palpitation, sweat gushing out of every pore, and too many other calamities to list properly.

---

* Excerpted from A. King, *The Drug Experience*, David Ebin (ed.), New York, N. Y.: The Orin Press, 1961. By permission Grossman Publishers, Inc.

Some of the psychiatric aides deliberately delayed giving us our drugs, pretending not to notice the agony tottering around them. They enjoyed their power and wanted to savor it. They were farm boys and had suffered callous authority themselves. Also, like everybody else including most of the doctors and all of the nurses, both male and female, they had a moral ascendancy over all drug addicts.

After seven days they stopped giving me even Dolophine and I instantly caught a cold. This is a standard development, as is vomiting, diarrhea and sleeplessness.

I stayed thirty days in Lexington and I never slept more than half an hour a night. The nights of the recently weaned drug addict are a special horror, because even after a few minutes' sleep his pajamas and his sheets are soaked with cold sweat.

After my last shot I was moved to another floor, among people who had already recovered. I had a roommate now, a mild, sentimental character from Chicago called Manny. Every Monday we had inspection. A really tough inspection. The men on the corridor spent most of Sunday evening polishing their floors, their windows and their furniture. Manny, too, proceeded to disembowel our room in a frenzy of cleaning and I tried to help him but I had to take time out for puking every few minutes. He was wonderful about it. Manny had a certain resemblance to Groucho Marx and this, I think, had early conditioned him to be something of a comedian. With great perception he recognized that I saw other virtues in him, so he gave up trying to be funny for me.

He was a husband and father who had long ago lost his family along the drug route. For a living he played small character roles in summer theaters and road companies. He too was a volunteer, but he meant to stay for the full six-month cure.

After vomiting for about ten days I was so dehydrated that I passed out in our room one day, so I was shipped back to the infirmary. . . . I was put to bed and given intravenous glucose, and I was sure that nobody in the whole world had ever been so deathly sick. I'll try to explain why it is so tough to cure a drug habit. When you take opiates in any but minute quantities, the body is shocked by these poisons and rejects them. This is normal. What is abnormal is to go on taking the stuff until the body is habituated to this toxic intrusion. The organism achieves this tolerance, finally, by altering the chemical constituency and balance of each of its billions of cells.

What Do You Think?

1. How would you describe this individual?
2. Would this description be effective as "anti-drug-use" propaganda? Why or why not?

2.   IS GROUP THERAPY THE ANSWER? *

Synanon is an organization that offers one approach to drug abuse. Basically it represents an attempt to allow individuals to find their own way back from drug abuse to a meaningful way of life. Although initially it treated only the narcotics addict, it now includes many people who abuse other drugs and also some people with other behavioral problems. The program is best described by the question-and-answer brochure produced by the Synanon Foundation.

What Is Synanon?

Synanon Foundation, Inc., is a non-profit California corporation. Incorporation papers were filed only 10 years ago.

Residents are involved in a full-time educational process—a life style which leads them to outgrow such stupid, anti-social behavior as drug addiction.

Today, Synanon is a full-fledged social movement.

What Does "Social Movement" Mean?

Synanon acts as a catalyst in communities where the Foundation has a house. Non-violent, free of drugs and alcohol and other psychic modifiers, completely integrated as a matter of course, Synanon offers these alternatives to strife seen in the larger society.

Persons from all walks of life find that conditions in Synanon lead them to communicate honestly, frankly, as human beings. Communication, in turn, produces the excitement and drawing power of creative acts—produces these both in the Foundation and the hosting cities.

How Many Residents Are There?

The first Synanon house, a shabby storefront in Ocean Park, had a population of slightly more than 30 persons. Today, there are more than 1,000 residents in a chain of first-class facilities reaching from coast-to-coast.

What Is The Synanon Game?

The Game is human beings sitting in a circle, seeing one another in small, extremely honest gatherings. It is Game-players in the act of cracking one another's false images with words, then talking about individual realities. It is human beings learning that we all—black, white, rich, poor, young, old—are the same deep inside and can learn from each other. Sometimes by yelling.

The Game is human beings getting rid of anger, frustration, remem-

---

* *Instant Guide to Synanon,* Synanon Inc., Oakland, California, (undated).

bered pain. It is the willingness of participants to change, to grow up, to gamble that they are good. It is learning that there is nothing to fear in the truth—and in expressing one's most basic convictions.

What Are The Rules? Who's In Charge?

Only one rule: no physical violence or threat of it. There is no official leader, no status-type to whom the others must play, though leaders will arise out of any human situation.

Is The Game Always Serious?

Not at all. It can be a lot of fun. There is much laughter, for life is funny, too, and the Game is an intensely concentrated life. Every life situation appears—the humorous among all the rest.

Who Plays The Synanon Game?

All Synanon residents. And non-resident members of the Game Club. Today, there are some 2,500 Game Clubbers throughout the country.

All kinds of people: architects, bakers, housewives, ghetto-dwellers, teenagers, vegetarians, millionaires, unemployed carpenters, movie stars, zoologists. From A to Z. Literally.

What Is The Synanon Trip?

A drugless voyage. The 48-hour, no-sleep sessions are held almost weekly at the Santa Monica house and once a month at the facility in San Francisco.

Generally there are between 40–50 participants (selected residents and Game Club members) on the Trip roster. Trippers all wear long white robes—part of the image-cracking plan.

Long Games, mood-peace ceremonies, mental activities, walks during breaks—all have important functions in the process of wiping away false barriers between people.

Does The Trip Change One?

After Trippers work through their own ego-pictures, they see the true equality between human beings. Humans see and accept other humans in strictly human terms—not as members of a certain economic bracket, religion, race, and so on.

A Trip breakthrough serves as a reference point: a person knows that old guilts, fears and half-baked beliefs need not control him. A new freedom to live and love is available. All the time.

Is A Trip Mandatory?

No. Choice is always present—before, during, after. The Tripper's OWN chemistry creates the new lease on life.

Who Operates Synanon?

Synanon has a board of directors. The Foundation President is an ex-addict named Jack Hurst (all executives come from within the organization) and Chuck is Chairman.

There are Division Managers, Game Club Managers, Department

Heads, Tribe Leaders, Kitchen Chiefs, Mail Girls—all the positions of a corporate structure, plus a few unique to what Synanon calls "The People Thing."

Who Does All The Work?

Everybody in Synanon has a regular job.

What Supports Synanon?

In part, commercial ventures operated by residents. Synanon Industries (advertising specialties) employs a big sales force and now grosses about $1 million per year. Texaco service stations run by Synanon have won awards consistently.

Another example of self-support is the Synanon Street Scene, a big fair held in San Francisco each year. Proceeds go toward making more room for new residents.

Any Outside Help?

Yes. Many services and a small mountain of goods are donated by friends in the larger community. A Supply Department at each house handles contacts and collections. Because Synanon is a tax-exempt organization, all gifts are deductible. What's more, addicts would be stealing thousands of dollars in goods and cash—to support their habits—if they were still outside the Foundation's life style.

Any Government Aid?

A little. For services in vocational rehabilitation in California, for instance. But Chuck will accept no contract with strings attached. This is the only way "the Synanon position"—honesty, integrity, self-rule, freedom to act as a loyal critic of government affairs—can be maintained.

How Else Does Synanon Affect Taxpayers?

On May 8, 1968, the Los Angeles Times ran a story about the rising cost of state institutions for drug addicts, alcoholics and the mentally ill. Andrew Robertson, Deputy Director for the California Mental Hygiene Department, is quoted as saying:

"The rise in admissions is expensive. It costs $75 to process a new patient at admission and $33.10 a day to care for him for the first 30 days. After that, the daily cost drops to $19.60."

In the same article, Dr. William Keating, Assistant Deputy Director, summarized the revolving door nature of some programs. "We're releasing more people," he was quoted as saying, "and we're getting more back."

Those are tax dollars. It costs about $3.80 per day to maintain an addict in Synanon.

How Long Do Residents Stay In Synanon?

Depending always on the individual and his progress, the usual time is between two-and-a-half and five years. Many residents choose to stay longer as Foundation employees. And some have decided to become Synanon careerists.

Why? Do They Fear Society's Stress?

It is a matter of personal choice, of values, of challenges. While Synanon graduates have gone on to make good in some highly competitive fields (television production, publishing, sales) other "eligibles" think the Foundation offers more creative and important outlets.

They believe in Synanon. They want to be part of the work that Synanon is doing in society.

Does Synanon Pay Salaries?

No. All needs are cared for, including those of whole families, from food and clothing to the most expensive kinds of operations.

The "good things in life" are not ignored. Good cars, television sets, books, home furnishings—all are available to residents.

What About Pocket Money?

After six months of residency, everybody gets $1 per week in WAM—walking around money. Every six months, there is a $1 increase until the ceiling of $5 per week is reached.

No one in Synanon gets more than the $5 a week.

Are There Only Addicts In Synanon?

No. Many persons with other behavior problems have come in to straighten out their lives. Due to the social movement aspect, Synanon is seeing another sort of resident, the apparently well-adjusted individual who simply prefers the Synanon life style. (One example: Northern Division Manager Bill Dederich would be making $30,000 a year if he took back his former business position in the large society. He is a non-addict who has examined his values and made a choice.)

How Does One Advance Through The Ranks?

In Synanon, it's not who you know, but what you do. Personal accomplishment, the ability to seek and assume responsibility, principles brought alive through action—these are the determining factors. "Character is the only rank."

What About Children?

Of course there are children born to married couples who live in Synanon. Often families are brought together again through the Synanon process.

There are nursery facilities at the various houses to care for the children of working mothers. Youngsters receive attention from the total environment.

Where Do They Go To School?

At the Santa Monica facility, the Synanon School runs from kindergarten to the eighth grade at present. Construction of a high school is in the works. All school personnel meet State of California standards.

Children not living in Santa Monica attend public schools, participating in [various] activities there as well as at the Synanon house in which they live.

Does Synanon Welcome Visitors?

Yes. Foundation facilities offer many activities for the public. Check the schedule at the nearest house.

What Are The Hours?

Synanon's doors are never closed. And in 10 years, there has always been coffee in the urns, around the clock. Peanut butter, jelly and bread are always out for sandwiches—a custom dating back to "the old days" when that was often all members had to eat.

Is Synanon Religious?

Not so far as specific denominations are concerned. Residents honor the faiths of their individual choices. It may be said that they follow Synanon principles religiously—that is, with a sense of dedication and faith in the process.

Any Final Comments?

"Synanon is a truly integrated community," writer John T. Wallace has observed. "A very practical place, too, since that which doesn't work for the benefit of residents and friends and the society is discarded along the way.

"The Foundation's effectiveness is a matter of record. You don't get these results with a frightened, inefficient, dishonest, irresponsible, selfish population."

About 2,000 persons have been admitted to the Synanon program, about half of whom have left without completing the prescribed course. Of the 2,000 an estimated 150–200 have actually returned to the community from whence they came.[1]

What Do You Think?

1. Would you recommend that Synanon centers be established throughout the country? Why or why not?
2. The account given above indicates that half of those who are admitted to the program do not complete the course. What reasons could you offer to account for this?

3. INNOVATION IN MENDOCINO *

Let the patients set the therapeutic scene. Next is a description of a somewhat unusual approach being tried in a state hospital in California:

[1] Excerpted from D. B. Louria, *The Drug Scene,* New York, N. Y.: McGraw-Hill Book Company, 1968.
* Excerpted from David Perlman, "Innovation in Mendocino State Hospital," *San Francisco Chronicle,* December 7, 1967.

The heroin addicts form a fiercely loyal therapeutic community up here; they call themselves "The Family," and together they have forged their own unique tools for psychotherapy.

The methamphetamine users here—meth heads, as they're known—are also creating an identity for themselves. They are the "Core Group," and they too see in group cohesiveness the hope for a future free of sickness.

Up until now neither prisons nor locked hospitals have blunted the menace of addiction. Theories abound, but no professional can say with certainty what causes addiction or drug abuse, let alone how to treat it.

Thus the green light is on for innovation, and no one has responded to the green light more avidly than Wayne Wilson, the hard-working social worker who directs the alcoholism and drug abuse programs up here at Mendocino State Hospital.

In view of the dismal record of failure in handling drug problems, Wilson asked himself, why not try a wholly new approach? His answer:

Let the patients, as the people who might possess the keenest insights into addiction, set the therapeutic scene. Forego locked doors, or rigid structure from above. Let patients experiment. Stop asking the pointless but traditional question: What is the proper role of the psychiatrist?

Wilson was backed by his boss, Dr. Ernest Klatte, the innovative, enthusiastic and wholly dedicated superintendent at Mendocino. Klatte says:

Most of us, in or out of hospitals, never function up to a fraction of our true potential.

If we impose external controls here it would simply serve as an excuse to these patients to avoid developing their own controls internally, to reject individual responsibility, to ignore their own potential. Addicts do that all their lives.

So we thought that if we could set up a scene that encouraged people to use their own ingenuity—a climate where people would be expected to behave appropriately—we might stop worrying about controls and instead find patients setting their own limits and learning to live within them.

What Do You Think?

1. Dr. Klatte states that "Most of us never function up to our true potential." Might this statement offer any insight into the nature of drug use? Does it suggest any possible solutions to drug abuse? Explain.

2. The advocates of this program state that the patients set their

own limits and then learn to live within these limits. What advantages would such an approach offer? Disadvantages?

4.   THE USE OF LSD WITH SEVERELY DISTURBED CHILDREN *

LSD has shown some promise of being useful in the treatment of very disturbed children. Here is a brief account from a scientific magazine:

LSD shows some promise of being useful in the treatment of severely disturbed children, so disrupted they cannot speak, cannot relate to people, and make continuous rhythmic movement, such as rocking back and forth or flapping their arms.

The drug's primary effect seems to be in making these children, who lack virtually all normal human responsiveness, more approachable. It also reduces their bizarre movements by more than half . . . Tentative findings are that the drug obviously helped the very disrupted, but it seemed to worsen the behavior of those in slightly better condition. This is still questionable, however . . . the first LSD administration might make a child worse, while the second might improve him.

But with very severe cases, LSD definitely made the children more accessible. Instead of avoiding contact, they would cling to the adult experimenter. They laughed and smiled more and could maintain eye contact.

What Do You Think?

How reliable is evidence such as the above? What else might you want to know in this instance?

5.   STOP THE PROBLEM WITH LAWS *

In the following reading, the Chief Counsel, U. S. Bureau of Narcotics, views the government's place in the drug problem.

The responsibilities of the Bureau of Narcotics relate to opium, its alkaloids and derivatives, the coca leaf and its principle derivative, cocaine, the plant cannabis sativa (marihuana), and a specific class of synthetics

---

* "LSD Helps Severely Disturbed Children," *Science News,* May 14, 1966.
* Excerpted from D. E. Miller, "Narcotic Drug and Marihuana Controls." Paper presented at National Association of Student Personnel Administrators Drug Education Conference, Washington, D. C. November 7–8, 1966.

called opiates, such as Demerol and Methadone. Many people think of narcotic addiction as something which has sprung up and which has become widespread in the last decade or two. The fact is that this is a relatively old problem. In 1914 Congress enacted the Harrison Narcotic Drug Act. . . . This legislation was followed by the Import and Export Acts of 1914 and 1922; the Act of June 7, 1925, barring the importation of crude opium for the purpose of manufacturing heroin; the Uniform Narcotic Drug Act approved in 1932; the Marihuana Tax Act of 1937; the Opium Poppy Control Act of 1942; an Act to control synthetic narcotic drugs in 1946; a Narcotic Control Act of 1956 and the Narcotics Manufacturing Act of 1960.

The Harrison Narcotic Act provides control over the distribution of narcotic drugs within the country. Registration and payment of a graduated occupational tax by all persons who import, manufacture, produce compounds, sell, deal and dispense or give away narcotic drugs is required.

The Narcotic Drugs Import and Export Act authorizes the importation of such quantities only of crude opium and coca leaves as the Commissioner of Narcotics shall find to be necessary to provide for medical and legitimate scientific needs. Importation of any form of narcotic drugs, except such limited quantities of crude opium and coca leaves, is prohibited. The importation of smoking opium or opium prepared for smoking is specifically prohibited. Likewise, the importation of opium for the manufacture of heroin is prohibited.

The Marihuana Tax Act also requires registration and payment of a graduated occupational tax by all persons who import, manufacture, produce, compound, sell, deal in or dispense, prescribe, administer or give away marihuana. The act is designed to make extremely difficult the acquisition of marihuana for abusive use and the development of adequate means of publicizing dealings in marihuana in order to tax and control the traffic effectively. . . .

The Narcotics Manufacturing Act of 1960 provides for a system of licensing and establishment of a manufacturing quota for all narcotic drug manufacturers, with appropriate safeguards with respect to the manufacturer of the basic classes of narcotic drugs, both natural and synthetic, for medical and scientific purposes.

The Uniform Narcotic Drug Act or similarly acceptable legislation is in force in all of the United States. The federal laws were never enacted as the only control necessary over the illicit drug traffic. It has always been contemplated that the authorities of the states will accept and discharge the primary responsibility of investigating, detecting and preventing the local illicit traffic conducted by the retail peddler, together with the institutional care and treatment of drug addicts within their respective jurisdictions.

The controls over marihuana under the Federal and State laws are similar. Under the Federal laws the Marihuana Tax Act of 1937 placed the same type of control over marihuana as the Harrison Narcotic Act of 1914 placed over narcotic drugs.

On the other hand, the States have covered marihuana within a definition of narcotic drugs since adoption of the new Uniform Narcotic Act of 1932. Legally marihuana is not considered a narcotic drug under the Federal law but is considered a narcotic under many State laws. In fact, the Supreme Court of Colorado has ruled that it is perfectly permissible to define marihuana as a narcotic drug.

What Do You Think?

1.   How effective can laws be in controlling drug use? Explain.
2.   Consider the effect of Prohibition on alcohol usage during the 1920's. Would the analogy be appropriate here?

6.   EDUCATION CAN HELP *

Here is a plea for less pretended "omniscience" on the part of adults and more efforts to listen to young people.

Education can help, education of ourselves and of the young people. This will have to be education *for* drug use, not solely *against* drug use. Ours is a drug-using society; as Sir William Osler said, "Man is a medicine-taking animal." We can tell them about drugs and what they do, what their dangers and benefits are. And we can expect some experimentation to result from our education. We can bring ourselves realistically and factually up to date on marijuana, LSD, DMT, and other psychedelic drugs and their effects. We can avoid putting out inaccurate, scare information.

At a recent conference on drugs in the schools, sponsored by the California attorney general and attended by teachers, police, and others, this problem came out again and again. The teachers pleaded for facts, real facts, to tell their students. The teachers had been using official police information that described marijuana and LSD as dangerous narcotics. Their students would come in with excerpts from basic literature, such as Goodman and Gilman's *Pharmacological Basis of Therapeutics,* that directly contradicted the "official" sources. The students know from their own experience that the scare stories are not true, that the drugs are not narcotics or addictive.

---

* Excerpted from Joseph Downing, M. D. "Something's Happening," *Medical Opinion and Review,* Vol. 3 #9, September, 1967.

The result is that students no longer believe anything their teachers tell them about drugs. The teachers feel betrayed by "official" facts, and are equally uncertain and distrustful. If we are to have a real influence on drug use, we must know at least as much as the young people about drugs and their effects. I suggest that one way to begin is to put aside our robe of adult omniscience, then ask the young people what their experiences are, what they think can be done. I further suggest we attempt to find out what is happening in the teenage culture, why it was that *Time* magazine named the population under 25 years of age as 1967's "Man of the Year." For example, we could listen to our teenagers' records, what the singers are saying, what the teenagers are hearing from Dylan, Donovan, Simon and Garfunkel. We could send an expeditionary force, suitably disguised, to the teenage dance halls. We might go so far as to invite some teenage LSD users to talk with us informally.

We need to make two-way contact with this age group, the adjusted young people who have the same standards as ourselves, and also with the drug users, the juvenile offenders, the runaways. We need to hear, as well as speak. We must accept that they don't have any answers; they are uncertain, demanding, contradictory, often unreliable. By listening, by trying to understand, by showing that we care what they do and are not condemning them, we can make contact.

If we make contact and maintain it, then we have a chance to bring them to realization of their social opportunities and obligations. But if they don't, we can't force them. Like it or not, we must respect their decision to be different at the same time we expect them to respect our way of life and our differences.

What Do You Think?

1.   How can a greater amount of adult-student communication be brought about?
2.   This article argues that education can help. If this is true, what kind of education is needed?

7.   RESEARCH MUST BE BASED ON FACT *

The following is a statement made by former Attorney General Ramsey Clark:

Drug abuse control is impossible without scientific research and public education as well as law enforcement. The failure of any of the

---

* "The Many Difficulties of Drug Abuse Control," *San Francisco Chronicle,* July 23, 1968.

three will mean the failure of all. The youth of today won't believe old wives tales about drugs, but what they want is solid scientific information about the effects, information which is often lacking. We have seen from the past all too frequently that to try to enforce the law that people don't believe in, to try to enforce the principle whether it is vast disagreement as to truth is to endeavor to do the impossible. Enforcement must be based on research, research on fact, and fact translated into relevant law. Research is only beginning to know the truth about drug dangers such as brain damage and the mutation of genes. Science will develop more than 100 dangerous drugs within the next ten years in addition to those already available, naturally or synthetically. The danger of the use of the new agents, as well as those now available, must be identified and the public must be made aware of them before extensive use develops.

What Do You Think?

1.   Compare Clark's view with the argument presented in Reading 6. In what ways are they similar? In what ways are they different?

2.   Would you consider Reading 4 as an example of the "solid scientific research" that Clark desires? Why or why not?

8.   CONCERNED JUVENILE AUTHORITIES *

A remarkably comprehensive set of recommendations was proposed by the Juvenile Commission of San Mateo County, California.

First, establishment of a central index to collect statistical information regarding the continued involvement of youth in dangerous drugs and narcotics is needed. This information should be collected from law enforcement agencies, school districts and private medical practitioners. Second, a survey may be made of all high schools in the county to assess the degree of drug use. Third, a request to the legislators of the county that reasonable action be taken to review the laws and penal sanctions as they relate to drugs and narcotics. The goal of this recommendation was that the judiciary be given a greater discrimination in their sentencing powers, as well as to bring the penal sanctions into a more responsible relationship with each other and the penalties for other crimes. Fourth,

---

* Excerpted from the *Narcotics Inquiry Report,* San Mateo County (California) Juvenile Justice Commission, November, 1967.

that the legislators of the county introduce legislation and appropriate funds for professional and medical research on the effects of marihuana use. And fifth, that the Parents and Teacher Organization be requested to conduct an on-going program of education on the problems of narcotics and dangerous drug use by the youth in the country.

What Do You Think?

Compare the recommendations presented in this reading with those presented in Readings 5 and 6. Which particular argument seems most profitable to explore? Explain your reasoning.

9. THE PROBLEM IS PEOPLE *

A journalist has this to say:

Long before LSD became something you could sell newspapers with, and build freaky communities around, I knew a prof who experimented with the stuff, and with other hallucinogens like mescaline, at a large California university.

Last time I saw this fellow, I asked him this question knowing I could expect a level answer: "How dangerous is LSD?"

His answer, "As dangerous as the person who uses it."

His answer stayed with me. On reflection, I think it is a good answer.

It really doesn't make any sense to blame drugs for the things that people do under their influence. That's putting the cart before the horse.

When a guy gets all tanked-up on Panther Puree, and goes to the family chez and beats the bejabbers out of the old lady, are we to blame the booze, or some deep-seated streak of violence in the guy's nature? And is it not possible that he drinks because of that violent streak, which booze will abate in small quantities, but unloose in large?

The drug problem, too, is a problem of people, more than of chemical substances which are used by some folk who find life wanting and have a need to soup it up.

This is recognized in a 130-page teacher guide and source book called *Drug Abuse* which was distributed by the State last week to California schools. It is a document containing much sound sense.

Says the report: "The ultimate solution, if one exists, to the problem

---

* Charles McCabe, "The Problem Is People," *San Francisco Chronicle,* May 29, 1967.

of drug abuse rests not in the control of drugs, but in the development of human beings who are resistant to drug abuse.

"In the final analysis, education about drugs may be deemed successful only if it leads the young person to say NO when he is confronted with the possibility of drug abuse."

And the first step here, of course, is to cure the harm done by parents. Parents have more to do with the conduct of addicts than drugs. Just as they have more to do with the conduct of homosexuals than perversity.

This question of unacknowledged parental guilt is a prime matter. The guilt makes faulted parents impregnable to the appeals of logic, makes them unable to admit that their emotions and their handling of their children, may be the real offender.

The shaken, insecure kid who turns to some form of moral analgesic most often does so not from the wicked fascination of drugs or booze, but because he has been bequeathed a faulted nature by his inheritance and upbringing.

In some cases, parents should doubtless be in favor of drugs, rather than against. They provide a way for weak children to cope, somehow, even if it is weak coping. If some kids weren't turning on with grass, they might be cutting throats.

The hardest of all truths for parents to face is this: If your kid commits murder, you can't blame murder for the crime. You can blame some violent defect in his nature. This violent defect is something you could have seen, and could have remedied or mitigated, if you had really been what you always think of yourself as: A good parent.

If your kid is a junkie, don't blame the backstreet pushers, or the Mafia, or the newspapers, or the fuzz, or Timothy Leary, though all of these play a part. The trouble your kid is in, if he's a junkie, is trouble that began at home.

What Do You Think?

1. Is the drug problem a problem of people? Why or why not?
2. McCabe implies that drug problems begin at home. Would you agree? Why or why not?

10.   A NEW APPROACH BY A SCIENTIST *

Dr. E. Leong Way, a noted researcher in narcotic addiction and student of drug abuse, makes an appeal for a radically different approach.

---

* Personal communication to the author.

I feel that the penalties associated with drug use should be tied to the *actions* of the drug user rather than to the drug he is taking. As we don't punish the social drinker or the Dexedrine user so we should not punish the user of marihuana unless, of course, his or her actions represent an intrusion on society. This intrusion would be the same no matter what the drug.

This statement is not meant to suggest that the laws governing the selling and distribution (pushing) of drugs be altered.

What Do You Think?

1. Would you agree with this author? Why or why not?
2. Would Way's argument imply that a person could legally use any drug, as long as in doing so he does not intrude upon society? Explain.
3. What sorts of reactions might the above argument bring?

11. AN OVERVIEW OF POSSIBLE CONTRASTS *

Finally, we have an over-all look at possible controls or at least the question of controls by an individual familiar with many of the recent attempts to affect such controls.

Those in favor of hallucinogenic drug use contend that it falls within an individual's constitutional rights that a person should be permitted to use chemical, as well as other means of conscious alterations, in the pursuit of religious experience, self-understanding and pleasure. Specifically they contend that prohibition violates the first amendment's guarantee of religion, and more generally that it is an unwarranted invasion of privacy, the basic right to be let alone as set forth by the 14th Amendment. They argue further that any harmful effects are confined to the individual, that society is not suffering directly and that legal attempts to protect an individual from himself are basically unworkable. The issue is one of prohibition and not regulation. The Constitutional right of the government to regulate drugs in the public interest is not questioned.

Several Supreme Court rulings made before and after the Volstead Act pertain to the issue of individual freedom vs. the protection of society from the harms of alcohol use [the Volstead Act is one of alcohol prohibition].

---

* Excerpted from W. H. McGlothlin, "Cannabis: A Reference," *The Marihuana Papers,* David Solomon, ed., Indianapolis, Ind.: The Bobbs-Merrill Company, Inc., 1966.

It is argued that as the liquors are used as a beverage and the injury following them, if taken in excess, is voluntarily inflicted and is confined to the party offending, their sale should be made without restrictions, the contention being that what a man shall drink equally with what he shall eat is not properly a matter for legislation.

There is, in this position, an assumption of a fact which does not exist, that when the liquors are taken in excess the injuries are confined to the party offending. The injury, it is true, first falls upon him, but as it leads to neglect of business and waste of property and general demoralization, it affects those who are immediately connected with and dependent upon him.

In another decision the Supreme Court stated:

The ultimate legislative object of prohibition is to prevent the drinking of intoxicating liquors by anyone because of the demoralizing effect of drunkenness upon society. The state has the power to subject those members of society who might indulge in the use of such liquor without injury to themselves to a deprivation of access to liquor in order to remove temptation from those whom its use would demoralize.

Roy Bates, in an article entitled "Psychedelics and the Law," summarized the opposing viewpoint.

"Freedoms, it is understood, have a pathology of their own. They can be reveled in unwisely; that's a private affair. They can be abused to the detriment of public safety; then the law must be on hand to curb them. But they ought not to be legislated away as if adults were children of an over-anxious mother."

Of course the above Supreme Court interpretations were made before the prohibition experiment failed and it does not follow that the prohibition of hallucinogens would be ruled unconstitutional on the same grounds. If, as I have argued, the principal social impact of hallucinogens is on the personalities and values of the users, the court might be asked to rule on whether the state has the right to protect itself against a chemical assault on its value system. A threat that might, if sufficiently widespread, endanger the social order.

The Supreme Court has never ruled on the constitutionality of state laws prohibiting the American Indians' religious use of peyote, but state Supreme Courts have overturned virtually all of these laws. In the most recent cases of Arizona and California the state contended that where religious practice conflicts with public health, that is the Mormon's practice of polygamy, the religious practice must yield. The courts, however, ruled the state must show that the practice is frustrating a compelling interest of the state before it can justifiably abridge the guarantee of religious freedom, and in the court's decision the state had not so shown the case of the Indians use of peyote. The decision was based entirely on the issue of religious freedom; as for other uses of peyote, the California Court stated that we do not doubt that even though technically peyote is a hallucinogen rather than a narcotic, the state, pursuant to the police power, may prescribe its use. It would perhaps be premature to conclude that the California Courts would sanction the religious use of LSD and other hallucinogens by non-Indians. The Indians at least had the precedent of a long cultural history on their side. Peyotism is the commonest religion among the American Indians. Religious use of peyote dates back to at least 1560 with an established church for the past fifty years. They use peyote within a highly prescribed religious ritual and they are of primitive culture with very little impact on society as a whole. Nevertheless, the California decision did not rule out the use of peyote by non-Indians stating the trial courts will have to determine each instance with whatever evidence is at hand whether or not the assertion of a belief, which is protected by the first amendment, is in fact a spurious claim.

Constitutionality is not the only question that is involved in a rational approach to drug control as the prohibition era so vividly demonstrated. The Harrison Narcotic Act sharply reduced narcotic addiction but created serious new social problems. Among students and certain other groups the marihuana laws are increasingly being regarded with a kind of disrespect that followed the prohibition of alcohol. Prohibiting the stronger hallucinogens may create even more disrespect, especially among users who associate their use with various socially sanctioned benefits.

In rationally examining the consequences of legal repression as a method of drug control we should consider: 1) the consequences of unrestricted use or non-punitive controls; 2) whether the laws are enforceable; 3) whether the prescribed punishment is commensurate with the offense, which is to say, whether it is consistent with that imposed for other offenses; and 4) the value of deterrence vs. the laws' unintended side effects.

On the first point, we already know a great deal about the social effects of the unrestricted use of alcohol. Alcoholism is generally attributed to previously existing psychopathology or social alienation. The basic question is whether, if alcohol were unavailable, problem drinkers would simply resort to equally deleterious outlets. A corollary to this question is whether legalizing such a drug as marihuana would compound social problems by increasing the numbers of persons using drugs to excess. If those who abuse marihuana were drawn from the population of alcoholics, there is sound argument for expecting an improvement in the social situation, at least in terms of the resulting physiological damage. It is true that few persons use both drugs to excess. On the other hand, it has been argued that alcohol and marihuana satisfy different needs and resulting abuse would be additive. The strong hallucinogens are not suitable for producing the continued intoxication that is possible with alcohol and marihuana. While it is too early to adequately assess the capacity for abuse of the strong hallucinogens, there are some reasons to believe that it would be fairly minimal for adults but appreciable among the less restrained younger group. By abuse, I mean primarily repeated use resulting in an undesirable personality affect.

Regarding the second point, the enforcement of LSD prohibition will certainly produce some formidable problems. Considering that one ounce of the colorless, tasteless, odorless liquid is sufficient for 300,000 doses. It is much easier to smuggle LSD than heroin or marihuana. And prosecution at the seller level will have more influence on price than on availability. The possibilities for concealment such as absorption on a page of a book or a piece of a cloth make it impossible to enforce laws against possession.

On the third point, the gross inconsistencies in the laws controlling drugs are undeniable. For instance, peyote, mescaline, LSD and psilocybin are virtually indistinguishable in their psychic effects but the patchwork California laws permit peyote for Indians, define mescaline as a narcotic and impose the same severe penalties as for heroin use, treat LSD as a dangerous drug with a misdemeanor charge for possession and do not cover psilocybin. At the same time marihuana, so mild a hallucinogen that it cannot be logically included in the above group, is treated as a narcotic with some violations requiring mandatory prison sentences of five to ten years. To add to this confusion, the consumption of alcohol is promoted with the full power of American advertising; and the illogic becomes rather appalling.

On the final point, we ask to what extent legal repression will deter the use of hallucinogens and how this is balanced against the law's unwanted side effects. Some argue that outlawing drugs that are considered relatively harmless may merely enhance their attractiveness among rebellious young groups. While this may be true, there can be little doubt that, overall, laws that are enforced reduce drug usage. Availability is a precondition for use and easy availability without legal complications will result in more widespread use than will occur under illicit conditions. Even the widely flouted prohibition laws are acknowledged to have reduced the total alcohol consumption (although perhaps not the total abuse), and the strikingly higher rate of narcotic addiction among members of the medical profession over that for the general population attest the effectiveness of narcotic laws in reducing overall usage.

It is important to ask not only how effective a law is as a deterrent, but also, who the individuals are who do not conform. Persons breaking the law on opiates come very largely from socially and economically deprived groups who demonstate a high rate of deviancy in non-drug areas. Until recent years the use of marihuana was also largely confined to these groups (except for jazz musicians). In the last few years there has been a rapid spread of marihuana use to college students and various other middle and upper socio-economic groups who have not heretofore had a general pattern of deviance. LSD was introduced into society through scientific and medical sources, and, up to now, has apparently not spread to the lower social groups. This combined with the fact that many persons using LSD are seriously motivated by hopes of solving personal problems or achieving some other lasting benefits means that a substantial number of the persons violating LSD laws will not be deviant in other respects.

This situation may lead to several undesirable side effects. First, some students and other persons who are not basically anti-social will suffer arrest, records, social stigma and other personal harm. Second, it leads a sub-culture with hostilities to the law which may generalize to secondary patterns of deviance. Third, it creates and supports organized crime as a source of supply. Fourth, it causes poor quality control of the drug which may result in overdoses or poisonous adulterations. Lastly, persons needing medical attention as a result of drug-induced reactions may not apply for it because they fear arrest.

Selective enforcement is another problem with drug laws that do not have the full support of the population, courts and police. The marihuana laws are frequently not enforced because the highest penalties are in poor social perspective. Police frequently overlook student use of the drug and the courts decline to prosecute. At worse, this situation can supply law enforcement agencies with a lever to attack other types of behavior that are unpopular but not illegal; at best, it results in gross inequality of treatment between certain lower classes under close surveillance of the law and students and upper socio-economic groups who may use the drugs with virtual impunity.

What Do You Think?

1. Might legal restrictions be a possible stimulus to even greater drug use (by way of the inevitable attraction of "forbidden fruit"), or is the opinion of state and federal governments of sufficient influence that it will discourage drug use? Explain your reasoning.

2. Can legislation against drugs possibly affect the person already well established in drug use? Explain.

3. Does the government have the right to legislate in this matter? i.e., is drug use within the domain of government concern, and are its consequences severe enough to warrant intervention?

4. Should drug use be deterred at all? Might people come to the

same conclusions about the matter whether drug use is discouraged or not?

5.   If drugs were openly available, would drug use be increased or decreased?

ACTIVITIES FOR INVOLVEMENT

1.   Listed below are a number of arguments for and against using drugs:

FOR	AGAINST
a. One's sense of awareness is heightened. Tasting, seeing, hearing, smelling, and touching become very intense.	a. It is against the law. Many people will suffer arrest, police records, and social stigma.
b. One is able to think at much deeper levels. Perception is increased. Relationships previously unnoticed are now discovered.	b. It can lead to withdrawal from, and failure to contribute to, society.
c. People become much more effective in coping with their environment and in solving their personal problems.	c. It leads to the support of organized crime as a source of supply.
d. Self-understanding is increased as well as one's ability to understand others.	d. It may lead to delusions, paranoia, acute withdrawal, excessive anxiety, nervousness, and other negative psychological and physical effects.
e. It is a very pleasurable experience.	e. It develops in individuals a tendency to forego responsibility for their actions.
	f. It may lead to the production of deformed children.

Hold a class discussion on the strengths and weaknesses of each point, both pro and con. To what extent would the validity of each point depend on the *kind* of drug being considered?

2.   Review all of the readings presented in this chapter. Which of the things suggested or being done with drugs seem most worthy of endorsement? Explain. What other possibilities can you suggest that might be done?

3.   Educated people are supposed to make informed, rational choices and not be swayed by emotional appeal or peer pressure. To what extent is the "drug scene" a result of emotionalism? Write two editorials for an imaginary newspaper, one in which you argue in support of this point and one in which you argue against the point. Be sure to explain clearly your reasoning in each instance.

4.   Listed below are two rather distinct views on the use of marijuana by teen-agers:

a. There should be no restrictions whatsoever. The laws prohibiting the smoking of marijuana should be repealed. Anyone who wishes to obtain "pot" should be able to obtain it merely by visiting a nearby drugstore.

b. The smoking of marijuana is against the law and is psychologically dangerous as well. Stronger laws, imposing ever heavier penalities, are needed.

Review several of the readings in this book and do some library research to see what evidence you can obtain to support or refute either of these views. Which seems most valid (if either), and why? Would you offer another alternative? Explain.

5.   What about the laws concerning drugs? How effective are they? To what extent are they needed? Should they be revised or abolished? Listed below are three viewpoints on these questions:

a. There should be no legal restrictions at all. Legal prohibition of drug use violates an individual's constitutional rights—specifically, the First Amendment's guarantee of religion and, more generally, the basic guarantee against an unwarranted invasion of privacy as contained in the Fourteenth Amendment.

b. A few laws are necessary, such as generally permitting the use of drugs for "medical purposes." We don't know enough about the effects of drugs, either short or long term, to allow their unregulated use. Any laws which are passed, however, should be drawn up in consultation with physicians and other individuals well aware of drug effects. Any laws already in existence should be reviewed by a panel of such experts to determine whether they should or should not be altered or repealed.

c. Strict laws, outlining in detail who, when, how, and where drugs may be used, and the penalties involved for improper acquisition and use, are essential. We cannot afford to take a chance on even the slightest possibility that drugs may harm people physically or psychologically.

Have students roleplay three individuals, each of whom holds one of these views, discussing the matter. Then hold a class vote as to what (if any) kinds of laws are needed. Allow informal discussions among individuals holding different views to occur before the voting.

6.   Listed below are several effects which various people have suggested may occur as a result of drug use. Place a YES in front of any that you believe is supported by definite evidence; place a question mark (?) in front of any about which you feel the evidence is contradictory; and place a NO in front of any that you feel is definitely not supported by any evidence:

——   Increased awareness of one's surroundings.
——   Heightened anxiety.
——   Greater friendliness and love for one's fellows.
——   Withdrawal from society.
——   Greater promiscuity.
——   Physical deterioration.
——   Mental deterioration.

—— Hallucinations.
—— Uncleanliness.
—— Damage to future generations.
—— Uncontrollable physical violence.
—— Disorganization of space and place. No control of time.
—— Feeling of being "in another world."
—— Disease.
—— Decreased desire for material possessions.

Use the readings in this book, and the bibliographic and other sources to support your ratings. Then rate each of the above-listed effects as positive (+), unsure (0), or damaging (—). Sum up the class's ratings and then ask your school newspaper (perhaps your community newspaper as well) to publish your conclusions. Include an explanation of why each point was rated as it was, what evidence exists in support of each rating, and the views of those who dissented.

7. How should we deal with the drug problem in the future?
   a. Wait and see what happens in the future before we decide?
   b. Pass more restrictive laws, as soon as they can be drawn up?
   c. Legalize the use of drugs for those addicted?
   d. Install a program of *voluntary* education on drugs and their effects in all of the elementary and secondary schools in the country?
   e. Install a program of *compulsory* education on drugs and their effects in all of the elementary and secondary schools in the country?
   f. Establish a national series of television programs to suggest to people a variety of ways by which they can enrich their personal lives without resorting to drugs?
   g. Establish a number of information agencies throughout the country to inform the general public about drugs and their effects?

Discuss each of these suggestions in turn, determining which would and would not be most effective, and why. What other possibilities can you suggest?

GLOSSARY

GLOSSARY

Acid: See LSD.

Acid-head: A user of LSD.

Addict: An individual addicted to a drug. See addiction.

Addiction: Compulsive drug use, characterized by overwhelming involvement with using and securing a drug, and with a high tendency to relapse after withdrawal from its use.

Amphetamines: A large class of drugs giving effects characterized by increased animation, euphoria, tremors, and other sympathetic nervous system signs.

Artillery: Material used for injecting drugs.

Bale: A pound of marihuana.

Bang: To inject drugs.

Barbiturates: A large class of chemically related compounds which are capable of a generalized depression of the body, particularly the brain. The effects become greater with increasing dose. These compounds are addicting.

Bennies: See amphetamines.

Benzedrine: Stimulant drug. See amphetamines.

Bhang: See marihuana.

Big C: See cocaine.

Blasted: To be intoxicated by a drug.

Blow one's mind: To break with personal reality.

Blow a stick: Smoke a marihuana cigarette.

Blue heavens: Amytal (a barbiturate—Amobarbital).

Blue velvet: A combination of paregoric and antihistamine for intravenous use.

Bombita: Amphetamine for injection.

Boo: See marihuana.

Boost: To shoplift.

Bummer: Bad drug experience.

Busted: To be arrested.

Cannabis: See marihuana.

Cannabis sativa: The flowering plant from which is derived marihuana.

Can: Approximately an ounce of marihuana.

Candy: See cocaine.

Cap: A packet of heroin.

111

Cartwheels: See amphetamines.

Charlie: See cocaine.

Chat: See khat.

Cocaine: A bitter, crystalline compound obtained from coca leaves that produces euphoria.

Coke: See cocaine.

Cold turkey: An abrupt withdrawal from narcotics.

Come down: End of a drug experience.

Cooker: Receptacle for heating drugs before using intravenously.

Cop out: Withdraw.

Deck: A packet of heroin.

Dexedrine: An amphetamine type drug. See amphetamine.

Dexies: See dexedrine.

Dexamyl: Drug containing dexedrine and the barbiturate amytal. Syn.: **Xmas trees.**

Dime bag: $10 worth of drugs.

DMT: Chemical (N,N-dimethyltryptamine) related to the hallucinogen psilocybin.

Dolly: Methadone (dolaphine).

Doriden: Drug similar to the barbiturate in action but of a different chemical structure. Syn.: **Goofers.**

Drop: To take drug by mouth.

Drug: Any substance that by its chemical nature alters structure or function in the living organism.

Fix: An injection of drugs.

Flip out: To lose mental control after using drugs.

Floating: To be intoxicated by drugs.

Footballs: A combination of dextroamphetamine and amphetamine.

Fuzz: Police, narcotic agents.

Ganja: Superior grade of marihuana.

Gin: See cocaine.

Give wings: Inject somebody with heroin by vein.

Goofballs: See barbiturates.

Grass: See marihuana.

H: See heroin.

Habituated: A state of mind in which the drug user (habitué) believes that the effects produced by the drug are necessary to maintain an optimal state of well-being.

Hash: See marihuana.

Hallucinogen: A drug capable of causing a large variety of psychic and perceptual changes including hallucinations, visual illusions, decreased concentration, changes in mood, and anxiety.

Hay: See marihuana.

Head—(pothead, acidhead):   An individual continually high on LSD, marihuana, or hashish.

Heavenly Blues: A type of morning-glory seed.

Hemp: Common name for the plant from which marihuana is derived (see cannabis sativa).

Heroin: A strongly addictive narcotic made from morphine.

High: To be under the influence of drugs.
Hooked: Addicted to drugs.
Horse: See heroin.
Hustle: To be a prostitute.

Intravenous (IV): Directly into the vein.

Joint: See marihuana.
Joy pop: Intermittent use of heroin by a non-addict.
Junkie: A narcotic addict.

Khat: A drug derived from an Ethiopian plant, Catha edulis, which has stimulant properties similar to those of the amphetamines.
Kick the habit: To stop using drugs.

Lid: Approximately 1 ounce of marihuana.
Lit up: Under the influence of drugs.
LSD: An extremely active hallucinogenic drug derived from the wheat rust fungus commonly called ergot. (LSD-25, lysergic acid diethylamide)

Mainline: Intravenous injection of drugs.
Marihuana, marijuana: Drug derived from the flowering tops of hemp plants which when smoked or taken orally leads to a dreamy state of altered consciousness.
Maryjane: See marihuana.
Mescaline: The active hallucinogenic drug found in the American cactus (Aztec name: peyotyl).
Meth: See methedrine.
Methedrine: Amphetamine derivative (see amphetamine). Addicting. Syn.: **speed, crystal, crink.**
Methhead: Chronic, heavy user of methedrine.
Morphine: A drug extracted from the opium poppy plant. Addicting.
The man: Police, narcotic agents.

Narcotic: Pain-relieving and sleep-producing drugs of the morphine type. All are addicting.
Narks: Slang term for the law enforcement officials concerned with narcotics abuse.
Nembutal: A barbiturate. Syn.: **yellows, yellow hornets, yellow jackets, nemmies.**
Nickel bag: A $5 supply of drugs.
Nod: To behave in a sleepy or lethargic manner.

OD: Overdose of narcotics which may be fatal.
Opiate: Any narcotic drug similar to morphine in action.
Opiod: A drug similar in action to the opiates but having a chemical structure unrelated to morphine.
Opium: Crude extract from the poppy plant from which the narcotics morphine, etc. are refined.
Outfit: The materials and equipment used by an addict to inject a drug intravenously.

Pack: A packet of heroin.
Panic: A scarcity of drugs.
Physical dependence: An altered physiological state produced by the re-peated administration of a drug, which necessitates the continued ad-ministration of the drug to prevent withdrawal symptoms.
Pot: See marihuana.
Preludin: Phenmetrazine, a stimulant drug similar to the amphetamines and used particularly in Europe.
Purple hearts: Phenobarbital (luminal). See barbiturates.
Pusher: Seller of drugs.
Psychedelic: Able to alter mental perception. Syn: hallucinogenic.

Qat: See khat.

Rainbow: Tuinal (amobarbital and secobarbital). See barbiturates.
Red birds, red devils, reds: Seconal (secobarbital). See barbiturates.
Reefer: Marihuana cigarette.
Roach: Marihuana cigarette butt.

Score: To obtain drugs.
Seconal: A barbiturate. Syn.: **reds, red devils, red birds.**
Shoot: To take drugs by needle (intravenously).
Shooting gallery: A place to take drugs by needle.
Skin pop: Inject drugs under the skin.
Smack: See heroin.
Snipe: Marihuana cigarette butt.
Snort: To take drugs by sniffing through the nose.
Snow: See cocaine.
Speed: See methedrine.
Speedball: Heroin together with cocaine or an amphetamine.
Speed freak: A person constantly high with amphetamine.
Spike: An intravenous needle.
Spoon: A measure of drug being used (usually about 1 gm. of amphetamine).
Stick: Marihuana cigarette.
STP: An hallucinogenic drug closely related chemically to the amphetamines and similar in its action to mescaline.
Sweets: See Preludin.

Tea: See marihuana.
Teeny-bopper: A teen-age hippie out for kicks.
Toories: See tuinal and barbiturates.
Tolerance: Development of a decreasing effect after repeated doses of a drug.
Toxicity: The quality of being poisonous.
Tranquilizer: Any drug capable of calming or quieting the emotional state of a patient without affecting clarity of consciousness.
Twenty-five: See LSD.

Weed: See marihuana.
Wired: To be addicted or habituated.

Yellow jackets: See nembutal (pentobarbital) and barbiturates.

BIBLIOGRAPHY
For Further Study

BIBLIOGRAPHY
For Further Study

Books

BISCHOFF, W. H. · *The Ecstasy Drugs* · Delray Beach, Fla.: Florida University Circle Press, 1966.

BLUM, RICHARD H. and ASSOCIATES · *Utopiates: The Use and Users of LSD-25* · New York, N. Y.: Atherton Press, 1964.

CHEIN, I. *et al.* · *The Road to H* · New York, N. Y.: Basic Books, 1964.

COHEN, S. · *The Beyond Within: The LSD Story* · New York, N. Y.: Atheneum, 1964.

DEBOLD, R. C. and LEAF, R. C. (eds.) · *LSD, Man and Society* · Middletown, Conn.: Wesleyan Univ. Press, 1967.

EBIN, D. (ed.), · *The Drug Experience* · New York, N. Y.: The Orin Press, 1967.

ELDRIDGE, W. B. · *Narcotics and the Law* · Chicago, Ill.: American Bar Foundation, 1962.

GOLDSTEIN, R. · *One in Seven: Drugs on Campus* · New York, N. Y.: Walker and Co., 1966.

KITZINGER, A. and HILL, P. J. · *Drug Abuse—A Source Book and Guide for Teachers* · Sacramento, Cal.: California State Department of Education, 1967.

LARNEI, J. · *The Addict in the Street* · New York, N. Y.: Grove Press, 1965.

LINDESMITH, A. R. · *The Addict and The Law* · Bloomington, Ind.: Indiana Univ. Press, 1965.

LOURIA, D. B. · *The Drug Scene* · New York, N. Y.: McGraw-Hill Book Company, 1968.

Mayor's Committee on Marihuana · Lancaster, Pa.: Jacques Cattell Press, 1944.

SIMMONS, J. L. and WINOGRAD, B. · *It's Happening* · Santa Barbara, Cal.: Marc/Laird Press, 1966.

SOLOMON, D · *The Marihuana Papers* · Indianapolis, Ind.: Bobbs-Merrill Co. Inc., 1966.

TAYLOR, N. · *Narcotics: Nature's Dangerous Gifts* · New York, N. Y.: Dell Publishing Co., 1963.

UHR, L. and MILLER, J. G. (eds.) · *Drugs and Behavior* · New York, N. Y.: John Wiley and Sons, 1960.

Articles

"Dangerous LSD?" *Scientific American,* February, 1966.

"Donna and the Sugar Cube" *Newsweek,* April 18, 1966.

"Fiedler Affair: Buffalo University Group Aims to Legalize Marijuana," *Newsweek,* June 12, 1967.

HAWKINS, M. E. · "Don't Dodge the Drug Question: Hallucinogens," *Science Teacher,* November, 1966.

"Keep Off the Grass?" *The New Republic,* June 17, 1967.

"Kick: Government Agencies Efforts to Stamp Out Drugs," *The New Republic,* April 16, 1966.

KLEBER, H. D. · "Student Use of Hallucinogens," *Journal of the American College Health Assn.* 14:109, 1965.

MCBROOM, P. · "Pot Penalties Too Severe," *Science News,* October 8, 1966.

MCGLOTHLIN, W. H. · "Hallucinogenic Drugs: A Perspective," *Psychedelic Review,* 6:16, 1965.

MCGLOTHLIN, W. H. and COHEN, S. · "The Use of Hallucinogenic Drugs Among College Students," *American Journal of Psychiatry,* 122:572, 1965.

"Potted Ivy: Alienated Students Smoking Marijuana," *Time,* May 19, 1967.

"Psychedelic Art," *Life,* September 9, 1966.

ROSENFELD, A. and FARRELL, B · "Spread and Perils of LSD," *Life,* March 25, 1966.

SANFORD, D. · "The Risks of Marijuana," *The New Republic,* April 22, 1967.

SPARKS, W. · "Narcotics and the Law," *Commonweal,* August 25, 1961.

"The Effects of Marijuana," *Time,* December 20, 1968.

"Turning It on with LSD: Doses to Mental Patients," *Time,* November 25, 1966.

UNGER, S. M. · "Mescaline, LSD, Psilocybin and Personality Change," *Psychiatry,* 26:111, 1963.

YOUNG, W. R. · "The Truth About LSD," *Reader's Digest,* September, 1966.

Films

LSD-25 (25 min; Color; San Mateo Union High School District) · Limited to only a consideration of LSD. Notes psychologic dangers of LSD use by individuals with preexisting mental problems. No mention of the chromosomal or birth defect damage which may occur with LSD.

Drugs in the Tenderloin (51 min; Color; prod. KQED-TV) · Vividly depicts the environment in which drug abuse occurs. Little of the effects produced by the drugs and their dangers.

Marijuana (34 min; Color; Bailey Films) · Discusses the physical and emotional dangers and the legalities surrounding marijuana use. Narrated by Sonny Bono (of Sonny and Cher).

The Losers (31 min; prod. CBS) · Deals with the personal, family, and community aspects of narcotic addiction but doesn't touch on the psychedelic drugs.

Escape to Nowhere (Approx. 35 min; prod. San Mateo High School District) · Excellent presentation of a real user's views on drugs and what they mean in her life.